Being Fair with Kids

The Effects of Poor Leadership in Rule Making

JIM DUECK, EdD

ROWMAN & LITTLEFIELD EDUCATION
A division of
ROWMAN & LITTLEFIELD PUBLISHERS, INC.
Lanham • New York • Toronto • Plymouth, UK

Published by Rowman & Littlefield Education
A division of Rowman & Littlefield Publishers, Inc.
A wholly owned subsidary of The Rowman & Littlefield Publishing Group, Inc.
4501 Forbes Boulevard, Suite 200, Lanham, Maryland 20706
www.rowman.com

10 Thornbury Road, Plymouth PL6 7PP, United Kingdom

British Library Cataloguing in Publication Information Available

Library of Congress Cataloging-in-Publication Data

Dueck, Jim, 1946–
  Being fair with kids : the effects of poor leadership in rule making / Jim Dueck.
    pages cm
  Includes bibliographical references and index.
  ISBN 978-1-61048-938-6 (cloth : alk. paper)—ISBN 978-1-61048-939-3 (pbk. : alk. paper)— ISBN 978-1-61048-940-9 (electronic : alk. paper)
  1. School age (Entrance age) 2. Readiness for school. 3. Academic achievement. I. Title.
  LB1133.D84 2013
  371.2'19—dc23
                                                                    2013011259

♾™ The paper used in this publication meets the minimum requirements of American National Standard for Information Sciences—Permanence of Paper for Printed Library Materials, ANSI/NISO Z39.48-1992.

Printed in the United States of America

This book is dedicated to
my brother-in-law, George,
for his talent in wordsmithing my thoughts,
and to my colleagues and friends in
Alberta's Learner Assessment and
System Improvement Groups for
their talent in assessment,
research, and accountability.

Contents

Preface

This is a book about a serious tragedy which we can put right with courage and determination. It is a call to action that identifies problems, defines them, and names them. It is not about theory, although sound pedagogic principles inform the solutions and rigorous analysis undergirds the critique. It is not about speculation and conjecture, although there are logical inferences and commonsense optimism about a preferred future.

My concern about unfair schooling practices began when I stepped into the classroom and saw firsthand the impact of unfair "rules" on our children. The arguments I make in this book had their genesis in the classroom and in my deep care and concern for the children in our schools. My research began in these early years as I taught and attended graduate school.

This interest grew and expanded during my years as a school administrator and then later when I became a superintendent and then team leader in a provincial ministry of education. Over the last ten years I have worked with leading educators in other parts of Canada, the United States, and Europe. Many of these individuals shared my concern about the issues I deal with in the book, and my ideas are shaped by their wisdom and experience.

The foundational research project, which was most relevant to the issues I address in this book, was one I oversaw during a twelve-year period as a senior leader in the Alberta Ministry of Education. Every year my team surveyed all the sixty-two school districts and compiled a large database on achievement. A K–12 student population of more than six hundred thousand students provided not only a large database but also an entire regional population. The statistical tests are based on carefully crafted surveys and tests, which meet the most rigorous statistical standards.

Upon retirement and in preparation for this book, I used a purposive sample and semistructured interview model to obtain qualitative information from key stakeholders. I discussed the findings of this research with teachers, administrators, parents, and trustees. During the course of my forty years in the education system I met with thousands of people to discuss issues and solutions around the subject of relative-age effect.

The primary research for producing the data was a team effort within Alberta Education, where staff in the Learner Assessment Branch and the System Improvement Group shared my concern and passion. The assembled data was distributed openly to and discussed formally with stakeholders, leaders in the department, and politicians. Sections within the story were not well-received by some stakeholders because they revealed ways in which students were systematically and systemically disadvantaged.

My years of interaction with educational leaders and my work in a senior government role led me to become increasingly sensitive to the need for our educational system to become more accountable and fiscally responsible. This became a major secondary motivation for writing the book. On the one hand, I remained primarily concerned about our children and the personal tragedy we are creating for them. On the other hand, I am also concerned about the fact that we are recklessly disregarding our young people as the greatest resource we have and we are doing this in a profligate way characterized by systemic waste and inefficiency.

The book begins with a description of the tragedy and a definition of the problems. Along the way I reference realistic and feasible solutions, but I develop these in depth in the last third of the book. Unfair schooling practices, which we knowingly ignore, are inexcusable, especially given the fact that there are reasonable solutions. And because the problems create a legacy of harm, they are unconscionable. My hope is that this book will encourage educators and noneducators to unite in a common effort to bring about the transformational change we need to ensure all our children are treated fairly.

Fairness to Students

OUR NATION'S MOST VALUABLE RESOURCE

Children are a nation's most valuable resource. They enter the world helpless, totally dependent on nurturing parents and other adults. Most spend a substantial portion of their childhood in a government-sponsored education system. Even when they enter their "first rite of passage" as schoolchildren, they remain essentially ignorant of the hopes and dreams adults have for them. Once in school they are surrounded by people who espouse commitment to helping them achieve their potential. Most progress through twelve years of primary and secondary education with relatively few setbacks and go on to experience varying levels of success in their personal and professional lives.

But a considerable number do not, and their story is largely untold and misunderstood. With so many resources and so much attention devoted to them, it seems inconceivable and even unconscionable that such a large group would begin to experience difficulties and even failure as soon as they begin formal schooling. Are there rules in place which can be changed to remove aspects of schooling which are unfair?

It is even more distressing to know that difficulties attributable to the school system frequently have a lifelong negative impact on a child. Apprehensions about these difficulties and enduring consequences lead to tensions between home and school as the adults involved endeavor to assess each child's potential and determine what educational, compensatory programming is required to address gaps between expectations and achievement.

Old, seemingly imponderable questions surface again, often in heated debate. "Isn't the system at fault?" "Can't we change schooling practices to ensure a far higher rate of success?" "Shouldn't we spend more to compensate for deficiencies in a child's home environment?" Are there answers to these questions which are reasonable and readily implemented? The questions even go so far as to tap foundational social issues, such as the appropriate age for starting school.

With a societal expectation that participation in the education system should be universal, the range in potential for academic success within an age cohort of students is significant. Tension emerges when schools seek to implement programs to address the differences in potential that surface, and debates about the fairness of opportunity erupt as gaps in success develop between children in a particular grade cohort.

All sides in the debate share a conviction that schools should address those gaps in a child's success which can be attributed to them. Social conscience dictates that decision makers need to assess the potential impact of their decisions on children and make informed adjustments that eliminate as many barriers to success as possible. Factors such as tradition, ignorance, entitlement, and change fatigue frequently result in resistance or at least reticence to adapt in the face of persuasive evidence.

This book argues that our love for children and our reliance on them for the future well-being of the country and world means that those forces and factors aligned against change must be respectfully and firmly resisted. When our educational decision makers refuse to change, in spite of evidence that shows we are subjecting a significant percentage of our children to a culture of unfairness, then forceful confrontation may be necessary.

POSITIVE OR NEGATIVE LEADERSHIP

Initiative for change typically starts with leadership, and it is axiomatic that all leadership makes a difference: the issue is whether that difference is positive or negative. In other words, leadership is not a neutral force in the change equation. The catalogue of unfair programs which follows in this book is largely the product of poor leadership—leadership that establishes rules which disadvantage children and contributes to their failure or disadvantage.

This book provides quantitative evidence that too many of our children enter their first "occupation" as students in our school system experiencing a distinct disadvantage caused by both an insufficient monitoring of their difficulties and then a failure to alter the system once the problem is discovered. For example, an ongoing disadvantage that has handicapped children for years, even though its impact is known and quantified, is the relative-age effect. In spite of persistent questions about its negative consequence, researchers have largely ignored the issue.

This means that until now there has been insufficient data to convince an apathetic public about the urgent need for change. It has also meant that educational leaders, who are generally aware of the problem, have done little to level the "playing field" in education for a significant percent of the student population. So marked has this lethargy been that it raises a question as to whether or not our society really values children as its most important resource. Rather than change how schools function, the educator's response has been to move children along using a practice known as "social promotion."

As a result, a substantial proportion of our children leave their first career with skill and knowledge deficiencies, along with an inaccurate view of themselves and the world in which they live. In short, they leave disadvantaged. This does not stop our educational leaders from professing, at least in public, their commitment to student well-being. Responsible queries result in defensive language from within the educational system about the lack of resources available to address limitless needs.

This pattern of blame shifting should not obscure the fact that the vast majority of educators are very committed to providing high-quality service to students within their sphere of influence. Generally they demonstrate that their work is not just a job, but a vocation. Teachers who embrace such a perspective obtain workplace satisfaction and a sense of reward from a genuine belief that their effort positively impacts students and society. For them, the primary concern is not about resourcing limitless need but about mobilizing parents to become active participants in their child's education.

Rule makers in the educational world tend to justify deficiencies in the system for nonmonetary reasons as well. To their way of thinking, flawed structures that provide for a relatively efficient and cost-effective education are to be preferred to an environment without structure or with less structure where costs would soar even higher and measurements of success would drop even lower. This is a valid concern and, like vocationally oriented teachers, there are many leaders who are doing their best to ensure that the masses of students are recipients of a quality education.

EDUCATIONAL CHANGE IS DIFFICULT

The dilemma is that once an operational rule is in place it inevitably becomes enshrined in the system and virtually impossible to replace. The slavish adherence to the existing school calendar is one example. It was devised for the agrarian era which provided for ten consecutive months of schooling followed by two full months of summer vacation to accommodate harvesting of crops. While some year-round schools now operate where break periods happen more frequently and for shorter periods of time, the vast majority of schools still operate on the agrarian calendar.

The impact of a long summer break on student success was unknown for a long time. There was anecdotal evidence indicating that teachers understood because they were undertaking significant review activities and reteaching in September—the first month in the new school year—in order to bring students up to curricular expectations for the new grade.

Uncertainty disappeared with the arrival of large-scale, standardized testing. Empirical evidence proved beyond a doubt that a school year, which focused on student success, required a revised school calendar. Today, many schools in our society operate with more frequent breaks during the year with a reduced time away from learning during the summer months. Nevertheless, the majority of school systems continue to function as though a student's forgetting rate is irrelevant.

A similar inability or unwillingness to adjust to empirical evidence can be seen in our education system's response to the data about the appropriate age for a child to enter school. The set of rules guiding the entry process usually establishes age groupings with the assumption that children are approximately six years of age. The age range within the group is usually twelve months, which is a significant period of time for six-year-old children. Hopefully, the data-story presented in this book will sufficiently motivate our educational decision makers to reconsider current rules. The disadvantages experienced by too many children can be overcome.

Fortunately standardized testing now provides quantitative evidence across the entire student population that enables rule makers to assess the impact of a twelve-month group approach on achievement. In essence, education is now experiencing a transformation where more decisions are being based on data or intelligence rather than gut-level responses or intuition. This transformation under way from the *age of intuition* to the *age of intelligence* is contributing to a more informed group of decision makers.

INTELLIGENCE INFORMS US

Of course, information challenges rule makers at all levels of the education system to consider, and in many instances reconsider, their practices. Unfortunately the rules currently in place may be so longstanding that even the existence of overwhelming evidence about inappropriateness is not sufficient to arouse rule makers to champion reform. In such cases, a shock and emotional discomfort may be prerequisites to new thinking and concrete action.

This book describes a cluster of interrelated failed practices, but its primary concern is with a practice that has students entering school with a twelve-month age cohort that encompasses widely varying levels of ability. This leaves many students in the cohort disadvantaged and in need of special assistance. Our society recognizes this reality and responds with what Michael Fullan called a "moral imperative" (Fullan, 2003) to help all who are needy and deprived.

Educators commit themselves to raising the achievement levels of all who are struggling in their class. Because the more capable students are not in need of special attention, their needs become secondary, which in turn consigns them to an achievement level below their full potential. It is a vicious cycle of failure created by a simple rule that requires students to enter school as a twelve-month cohort.

Focus groups of parents, teachers, school administrators, and school trustees were organized in preparation for this publication so that a qualitative story of meaning could be added to the quantitative record of definition and description. These groups were homogenous so that participants could express more freely in a context where their language and values were understood.

BIRTH MONTH AND IMMATURITY

Parent participants in the study were quick to express their concern about young children entering the school system when they are too young or immature to experience the pace of success exhibited by other students in their class. Parents readily understood a child's susceptibility to adopt a negative self-esteem when they observed the success of their peers in areas where they themselves were deficient. They recognized that children are sufficiently astute to understand where they stand relative to other children in their age group.

Teachers in the younger grades also recognized the significant relationship between birth month and academic success. Without seeing the quantitative evidence, teachers in their focus group stated that students born before September (the beginning of the school year in their environment but only two-thirds of the way through the January to December registration period) have better attention spans, are more interested in what is happening during school lessons, learn routines more quickly, and socialize better. In their experience there are easily recognized, age-based differences among children in the registration year.

One observation summarizes well the point parents and teachers were making, although in this case it was a psychologist commenting on the issue in a school district administrators' focus group. In his mind, students born near the end of the registration period, that is in the September through December period, were doing nothing "wrong" from a cognitive perspective, "they were just too young for the group." But the result for him was that he spent most of his time dealing with end-of-year birth-month students. Furthermore, this meant he had to spend most of his time with concerned parents helping them deal with the implications of their children being among the more immature in the group.

In summary, there are many immature children who enter the school system in September whose immaturity is not a factor of their environment or capacity, but rather the month in which they were born. Put another way, they are immature relative to others in the cohort simply because they are younger. They may not be immature relative to others born in the same month, but they may appear immature when compared with other children who might be eight to eleven months older. The age spread within a class of grade one students could be as great as twelve months or 16 percent of their lifetime.

This differentiation is significant to a six-year-old child. By way of analogy, segmenting children into year-long cohorts is like mother robins pushing all their babies out of the nest on the same day, even though they were conceived on different days. In the life of a baby robin, even one day can be the difference between flying and tumbling to the ground. A premature launch would be dangerous and fundamentally unfair to the younger baby robin. In the case of our children, a miscalculation of readiness is similarly deleterious, unnecessary, and unfair.

This book will demonstrate the degree to which we practice unfairness with a significant portion of our nation's most valuable resource. It will also demonstrate how this poor practice impacts other students negatively. It will conclude with a proposed solution—a relatively simple change in our educational system that will reduce costs substantially, reduce student failure significantly, and increase student achievement for the majority of the student population. Seldom is an initiative for improvement in education not accompanied by a request for additional funding. This book will do the opposite, and in the process offer a realistic solution that is relevant to schools in North America and beyond.

Birth Rather than Worth Counts Too Much

BIRTH MONTH IN SPORTS: GLADWELL

Many people are aware of Malcolm Gladwell's 2008 book, *Outliers*, in which the author describes the relative effect of age on athletic achievement and demonstrates why older children have superior skill development. The parallels between what he found in the realm of sports and what is to be found in the area of educational achievement are profound. His findings certainly underscore the benefit of family planning so that parents have their children born in the right months on the registration calendar. As a generalization, the talent of a child in sports is trumped by the relative-age effect when young children are organized into twelve-month groupings.

Gladwell's research uncovered the fact that a significantly disproportionate number of elite athletes were born in the first half of the registration year. He drew his statistics from an examination of the roster of a junior hockey team whose players were aspiring to play professionally in the National Hockey League (NHL). What he discovered was that the roster of the junior team that he was studying totaled twenty-five players, fourteen of whom were born in the first half of the registration year. Only six players were born in the last six months of the year, even though this period of time was twice the number of months.

Gladwell went on to examine the rosters of all the teams in the Ontario Hockey League and Western Hockey League. What he discovered was that there were more players born at the beginning of the calendar year than later. Thus, the same pattern held true.

Such a high degree of player participation in elite-level hockey for the earlier part of the registration year occurred because registration into programs is usually based on the calendar year, January to December. Further, utilizing a twelve-month window for recruitment resulted in a range in athleticism as well as in physical development. This left some young men significantly advantaged over others born in the same year. It is not too difficult to discover the nature of this advantage: older children are usually bigger, stronger, and faster than younger children with the result that they are selected at early ages to play in the more advanced leagues or tiers where, not surprisingly, they find the best coaches and resources.

Gladwell labeled this the "10,000 hour principle," by which he meant that older children had many hours of additional physical, emotional, and intellectual maturity that made it possible for them to develop more quickly. This had a cascading effect in their lives. Their "10,000 hours" enabled them to achieve at higher levels, which in turn placed them in higher tiers where they played with better players and were coached with better coaches. Consequently, the spread between them and the younger players in the same twelve-month cohort grew greater with each passing year.

Howerchuk's Hockey Lessons

In a related study which builds on Gladwell's research, Dale Hawerchuk, a retired NHL hockey player, recently posted on the World Wide Web a review of 720 Canadian-born players born from 1990 to 1994 who played in the NHL during the 2010–2011 season. In the 1990 cohort of players, approximately forty were born in the first quarter of the calendar year and another forty-five were born in the second. The number of players born in both the third and fourth quarters was in the mid-twenties in each quarter.

The highest number of Canadian players in the NHL during the 2010–2011 season were born in 1991, when more than one hundred and fifty players were born in the first two quarters compared with approximately seventy born in the last two quarters. Similar patterns for 1992, 1993, and 1994 demonstrated the clear advantage older players enjoyed over younger players born in the same year.

Hawerchuk's study provided clarifying evidence of the nature of the advantage experienced by older elite players in the same cohort year. While more of the older elite players reached the elite level, they did not outperform those who were younger. To demonstrate this, Hawerchuk analyzed the relationship between birth by quarter and the "points per game" (PPG) totals averaged over the number of games played. PPG has the advantage of neutralizing the difference in the number of players from each birth quarter by focusing on performance, which in turn taps the concept of "talent" or ability.

In the 1990 birth cohort, players born in the fourth quarter actually had a higher PPG than any of the other three quarters. There were mild variances in all of the years, but the generalization was that players making it onto the roster of an NHL team were fairly equal in their scoring prowess regardless of their birth quarter. The talent of those reaching elite status was, therefore, not explainable by the month in which a player was born. This suggests that the reason twice as many players were born in the first half of the year as in the second half was not a factor of talent, but of other causes which left the selection process flawed and many equally talented "second half of the year" hockey players disadvantaged.

We can illustrate Hawerchuk's conclusion in another way. Five very prominent Canadian-born hockey players over the past half-century—Wayne Gretzky, Mark Messier, Bobby Hull, Frank Mahovlich, and Mike Bossy—were all born in January. Gordie Howe was born in March, while Sidney Crosby was born in August and Mario Lemieux in October. Of the arguably greatest players in the last fifty years, only two—Mario Lemieux and Sidney Crosby—were born in the last quarter of the year. Lemieux and Crosby's birth months demonstrate that phenomenal talent is also evident in players born in the second half of the year.

Players born in the second half of the year may be naturally blessed with exceptional skills and/or superior size compared to those born in the first half, but these advantages are often muted and less likely to be recognized because the exceptional factors emerge later. There will be some who fit into the category of bigger, faster, and stronger. Disadvantages can be ameliorated by extraordinary environmental factors, such as parent support seen in early morning runs to the hockey rink and large investments in equipment, and unusual physical attributes of strength and coordination, but the normal pattern is one of continued disadvantage.

While writing this book and being further curious about the impact of birth month on a team, the player's list for the Philadelphia Flyers—a high-performing NHL team at the time—was examined. There were fourteen Canadian-born players on the team, eight of whom were born in the first two months of the year. Not surprisingly there were high-performing players on the team who were born in the latter portion of the year, but the majority were born in January or February.

Hawerchuk concluded his insightful work on the correlation between birth month and hockey stardom by undertaking one more study, this time on all the young Canadian men selected to play junior hockey over the period 1964–1984. There were 2,500 players whose birthdays were between January and March compared to fewer than 1,000 whose birthdays were between October and December. Being bigger, faster, and stronger early in their career development helped these young men achieve their goal of playing in the junior leagues and, ultimately, professionally in the NHL.

This research from the world of sports clearly demonstrates the advantage older children experience in the registration period. However, it also is clear that the birth-month effect is a generalization and not a rule. There are players born in the latter half of the year who earn elite status, and exhibit talent which is roughly equivalent to the other players. It is also important to note that the hockey world has a method for dealing with players it deems to be "inferior": it demotes them to lower tiers where they are unable to hinder the development of those destined to be "elite."

THE INTELLECTUAL BIRTH MONTH

Grouping children into one-year cohorts is a fairly pervasive practice in our culture even though people are able to see considerable variation in ability and recognize the disadvantage that results. Hawerchuk's research corroborates Gladwell's, and together they attest to the existence of a tradition or practice that imposes unfairness on children; the practices perpetuate this unnecessary and harmful result on all those realms in society that are based on our decision to group children into twelve-month cohorts.

Intellectual, social, and emotional development in a child parallels physical development. What is true in one domain is generally correlated with a similar reality in the other domains. In other words, development produces "winners and losers"—not because of ability or home environment, but because of artificially created immaturity arising from the month of birth.

Variations in maturity have a profound impact on what takes place in the classroom. Our educational system does not take grade one students and place them into tiers where there is no interaction with more capable students. We recognize that weaker students benefit intellectually from interacting with the stronger students because of the role modeling which occurs. It is equally important, however, to discover whether there is a negative impact on stronger students who are required to interact with less capable students in the diverse cohort. Previous research has been relatively silent on this issue.

Gladwell and Hawerchuk demonstrated how in team sports birth month is a significant element in success. This book will demonstrate the degree to which birth month is also a significant factor in classroom success. In these domains, birth rather than worth counts too much! Whenever a system that mandates universal participation disadvantages or degrades the worth of a significant number of participants simply because of a birth month, that system needs change. Our educational system is such a system.

Gladwell articulated the resulting unfairness succinctly and effectively:

> We could easily take control of the machinery of achievement . . . but we don't. Why? Because we cling to the idea that success is a simple function of individual merit and that the world in which we all grow up and the rules we choose to write as a society don't matter at all.

But rules written by society can be changed by society, and in ways that reverse the egregious effects of unfairness and disadvantage seen in such practices as twelve-month grade cohorts. At one point in the history of Western education, this was understandable. Empirical data justifying change did not exist. Just as no one could have anticipated the consequences for young hockey aspirants faced with a twelve-month registration window into hockey's establishment, so no one understood the unintended effects of an annual single-date entry system into education's establishment.

For too long our society operated in the *age of intuition* whereby people relied on their "gut instincts" and anecdotal evidence for determining rules. Today, we see the advent of the *age of intelligence* when we possess huge quantities of data and information which we must use to assess the rules we employ and the decision-making processes we use. The moral principles in education need to embrace fairness to students whereby their success is not impacted by birth month, over which they had no control.

In the education context, the recent advent of large-scale, standardized testing provides rule makers with a plethora of data demonstrating the ill effect of one rule, as well as how it can be altered so that our children, who really are our nation's most valuable resource, do not have to be negatively impacted for life. A single-date entry system is one of these rules which will benefit from reconsideration.

Changing longstanding practice is difficult, and our natural tendency to embrace order and stability and to avoid turbulence and upset for those with privilege, mean that change does not come easily. In the case of education, rule makers must courageously step forward to ensure that all children are treated fairly and equitably. Without acts of courage where ignorance, privilege, and complacency are confronted, the status quo will remain the modus operandi to the detriment of students and society as a whole.

Those advocating change need to keep in mind that there is a sense in which history is "valueless." Until people internalize truth and make it their own, usually through a journey of self-discovery, the ideas or concepts that represent truth remain meaningless. Once embraced, reform is possible and old tendencies to inertia disappear. Then what was learned in history becomes meaningful and of sufficient impetus to pursue reform with passion.

This book seeks to present evidence that encourages people to take constructive action. For those in positions of influence and decision-making authority, it is important because we only get one opportunity with an age cohort of students. It is clear that little is being done to create fairness in the world of athletics, perhaps because sports are not valued as a "right" for all individuals, but in the world of primary and secondary education a similar disregard for fairness is unconscionable.

The key points made in this chapter are:

- In hockey, as well as other team sports, a significantly disproportionate number of elite athletes are born in the first half of the registration year.
- Utilizing a twelve-month window for recruitment resulted in a range in athleticism as well as in physical development.
- The spread between older and the younger players in the same twelve-month cohort grew greater with each passing year because of ongoing superior coaching and higher levels of competition for older players.
- Younger players qualifying for the elite level of competition performed at the same level as their older peers and in the same age cohort.
- Relative-age effect is a generalization and not a rule.
- Development produces "winners and losers"—not because of ability or home environment, but because of artificially created immaturity arising from the month of birth.
- Education is experiencing a transformation from the *age of intuition* to the *age of intelligence*.
- We can change rules which can be proven to be unfair to our children.

Relative-Age
Effect in Education

NOT ALL PLAY IN SPORTS

Studies on the success rate of elite hockey players indicate that those born in the first half of the year have a significantly higher rate of participation than those born in the latter half of the year. Ability, on the other hand, was not associated with birth month because players making the cut demonstrated equivalent success. In other words, there may not be as many players numerically, but the quality of talent is similar.

Only a small portion of the population is involved because many children are not athletically gifted or motivationally inclined to play sports. This reduced the research population to an esoteric group, which was reduced further by the fact that all the players were male. This reflects the fact that elite hockey at the professional level is currently all male.

The culling-out process begins early in sports. In hockey, for example, most boys who eventually participate do not even lace up a pair of skates until after coaches have streamed their motivated and talented peer group onto elite teams. Most of these late starters never rise to the level of the early participants and leave competitive hockey before achieving advanced status.

The situation might not be as dramatic in other sports, but all of them identify the exceptional child at an early age. In the end, those who eventually become professionals are a very small percentage of the population. Along the way the average young athlete, the good athlete, and even the very good athlete are sidetracked into various, talent-based tiers where they continue to enjoy the sport before they either drop out to pursue other activities or settle for recreational play.

BUT ALL LEARN IN SCHOOL

By way of contrast, education requires virtually all children to participate within a specific age period. As in the case of athletic leagues, the registration cohort spans a twelve-month period, or one calendar year. Not only are all children expected to join a designated cohort, they are also expected to remain a part of it for many years and progress through a common curriculum before alternate pathways open up in later years. Even then they are expected to carry on until "graduation."

Every year students are expected to advance in accordance with a specified expectation in various curricular domains before they progress to the next level. This means there are many more expectations regarding universal participation in the intellectual domain, and with this expectation comes a complex array of compensatory programs and strategies to cope with variances in ability, motivation, and socioeconomic factors.

Parents accept that children differ from each other and that they mature at varying rates. Of course experiences and learning in the school further accentuate inherent differences. This leads people to attribute variances in student achievement to nature and nurture. This latter influence is frequently subdivided into categories such as parenting and pedagogy, which describes the close relationship of school and home in the maturation process of the child.

Western societies have shied away from efforts to control processes in the natural domain that shape and form the individual. Manipulating people through some form of engineering is generally thought to be reprehensible. In the nurturing domain, controls are often seen as acceptable, even essential. Grouping students into twelve-month categories for efficiency's sake is a case in point. The negative effects of this intervention are largely ignored because they are complex and not readily seen. Now, however, a large body of empirical data has brought to light the serious harm this social convention creates.

Now it is possible to understand the inappropriateness of "grades" as we have defined them for generations. When a student is designated as "grade three," too many assumptions automatically follow, and predetermined decisions and actions result. Most notably, all children tagged as "grade three" frequently are considered to be in the same instructional space at the beginning of the school year and are expected to end up near the same instructional space at year end.

Even as recently as the 1950s, teaching guides identified the instructional content for teachers on a specific date in the school year. While our educational system has become much more sensitive to the pace and style of the individual student, there remains a lack of awareness of how assumptions about grade level disadvantage individual children. Therefore, the vast majority of students continue to progress through the system at the same pace without conscious, intentional thought of what this means to students with widely divergent maturity levels.

All Are Not Ready To Learn

Associated with the concept of "grade" is the notion that all children are ready to begin their formal learning at approximately the same time. Therefore, most school systems in the world utilize an organizational rule which assigns a common date for students qualifying to enter the school system even though there will be a span of 365 days between the oldest and youngest students within the grade cohort.

The research community has paid little attention to the impact on outcomes that is associated with the maturity of children when they enroll or the span in age of the twelve-month cohort. Both of these issues are significant factors in student achievement and would benefit from greater analysis and discussion. This publication examines this neglected area and clarifies how the rules in place result in disadvantage for a significant number of students. Once the data is exposed and the unfairness is demonstrated, rule makers will be challenged to make changes and provide a more equitable learning environment.

It is incomprehensible to think that the education system could purposely continue providing unfair situations to a nation's most valuable resource. However, when a rule has been in place for so long—in this case centuries—it is difficult to replace it with an alternative. Peter Senge, renowned researcher on change and director of the Center for Organizational Learning at the MIT Sloan School of Management, once commented in an informal setting that achieving change in education was more difficult than in any other profession. We can explain this in part by the fact that the relatively low level of accountability in education results in little pressure from the stakeholders for change.

Another reason for the minimal pressure to change is that the issues often appear complex to a busy, preoccupied public, which is the case with the relative-age effect examined in this book. It is the case with other issues as well. For example, in February 2011, the *New York Times* wrote about the manner in which New York City's private and public schools introduced reading.

New York State mandates that public schools begin teaching reading almost from the first day of kindergarten, but private schools have latitude to establish their own curriculum. According to the *Times*, "Some of the most prestigious (private schools) choose not to teach reading until first grade or later. These schools' deliberate approach is causing friction."

What is this friction about and who is it between? One private-school headmaster commented to the media that, "Parents who get anxious think that education is like a race and you've got to get running fast, and if you don't you're going to fall behind and then you're going to lose the race." A headmaster in another private school demonstrated a differing perspective by indicating that staving off formal reading instruction in kindergarten "stops the growth (of a child) and could make education a potentially stultifying experience."

These different perspectives about the optimal time to begin instruction in reading leave a superficially informed public confused, uncertain, and unwilling to crusade for change. Given that relative-age-effect issues are significantly more complex than the appropriate time to introduce reading, it is understandable that there has been little pressure to change the rules about twelve-month grade cohorts.

On the other side of the continent in California, educators and decision makers were also grappling with the appropriate time to begin reading instruction. California, along with three other US states, allowed children to begin kindergarten in September in the year when their fifth birthday occurred as late as the following December. The *San Francisco Gate* reported teachers believed, "Children with fall birthdays are disproportionately recommended for intervention: extra reading instruction, summer school, private tutoring, retention, and even special education."

Once this became a recognized phenomenon in 2010, California rolled back the entrance date for kindergarten to September. Such action addressed part of the problem, but another problem of a twelve-month spread in maturity remains. In California's new system, October to December birth dates are simply now enrolled in the following calendar year to create a twelve-month span from October to September. Consequently, students will continue to struggle to keep pace. As long as there is a single-date approach to enrollment in a twelve-month period, there will always be a relative-age-effect problem.

The issue is not only the month in which babies are born, but also the differences in maturity across the cohort. The negative consequences of the relative-age effect arise from the fact that the cohort incudes children born over a twelve-month period and that they enter this cohort at one point in the calendar year. These two factors combine to create an intolerable environment of unfairness for our children.

The key points made in this chapter are:

- In sports but unlike schooling, those who eventually become professionals are a very small percentage of the population.
- Education requires virtually all children to participate within a specific age period.
- Students are expected to remain a part of schooling for many years and progress through a common curriculum before alternate pathways open up in later years.
- In school, a designated grade consists of multiple levels of student achievement.
- There is a mistaken belief that all children are ready to begin their formal learning at approximately the same time.
- Researchers have paid little attention to the impact on outcomes that is associated with the maturity of children when they enroll or the span in age of the twelve-month cohort.
- The issue is not only the month in which babies are born, but also the differences in maturity across the cohort.

4

The Annual Single-Date Entry

THE DOMINANT RULE FOR BEGINNING SCHOOL

There are many rules, conventions, and practices in education which guide its delivery and influence the degree to which students experience success. One such convention, which decision makers have codified into law in many jurisdictions, is the annual single-date entry system. It has remained part of the education system's set of rules for generations.

This rule is so dominant that educators plan virtually every other process around it, and its impact is felt in many other institutions and industries. Classes of students are organized after the first few days of school and rarely reorganized unless there is a significant shift in population during the school year. Even the educational terms "school year" and "grade" are based on the annual, single-date entry. Virtually all students progress to the next grade on the anniversary of their first entry date, which is usually September in the Northern Hemisphere.

There are two variations to the idea of a single-date entry that are noteworthy: the emergence of year-round education and the trend in the United States toward an August entry. This latter trend follows the same principles of the September entry but merely rotates the annual clock one month forward. Mandating that all students begin a new school year in September is so common in our society that September is almost as important for new beginnings after summer vacation as is the traditional "New Year" on January 1.

Anyone attempting to mess with the common idea that school begins around the beginning of September does so at their own peril. Change is seldom appreciated, much less supported. In this case, the collective memory is that every generation has dealt with the annual single-date entry phenomenon and parents have "always" planned their life around the entry date and automatically done whatever was necessary to make sure that their child was present and ready for the first day of school.

Schools, too, are firmly entrenched in the single-date entry ritual: class routines are established, administrators establish school routines around it, students form friendships with the entry in mind, and teachers organize their lesson plans with a substantial review of the previous year's forgotten learning in mind. The beginning of the new school year is actually the beginning of a new life.

The September 1 launch anticipates another idea, namely that the year is a literal year with a beginning and ending. So engrained is the understanding of school starting in September and ending in June, followed by a two-month break, that any other approach is inconceivable. Even when a school system is so bold as to innovate with the September entry, it does so within the conventional twelve-month protocol. Schools that start in August, rather than September, close in May rather than June. A two-month break follows, and a twelve-month cycle begins again in August. In schools which opt for a trimester or quarter system, the alternative organizational structure is still set with a twelve-month cycle in mind.

An Underestimated Moment in a Child's Life

To a six-year-old child, one year is a monumental period of time because it represents approximately 16 percent of his or her life. Physically, during a twelve-month window, they likely will experience phenomenal size changes in their clothing and footwear. These physical adjustments, which are recognized as a normal part of life, have to be accommodated in the family budget. Every parent understands this reality and makes financial plans to adjust to a substantial increase in family expenses.

There are no long-term negative effects of undergoing changes in physical development at different stages in life unless, as Gladwell records in his research, the child aspires to a career that relies on physical ability, such as is required of professional athletes. Participation in an elite athletic endeavor is related to variances in physical development but, for the vast majority of children, the reality of a twelve-month spread in physical development is merely a bump in their road to adulthood. Outside of the sports arena, few careers require extraordinary foot speed, height, arm reach, or physical strength.

When the focus shifts to the intellectual domain, every child is potentially affected, because every child attends school where the primary responsibility is the development of intellectual capacity. A child's development in the social, emotional, physical, and spiritual domains is the primary responsibility of the home, although the school shares some supportive responsibility in these important areas. Developmental delays in the intellectual domain are a serious concern for educators, because it is recognized that this domain is the school's primary responsibility.

The Pressure to Succeed

Parents express great pride and pleasure when their child is able to print their own name, count to one hundred, repeat in order the letters of the alphabet, read through a particular reader, and so on. Teachers feel the subtle and not-so-subtle pressure of curricular expectations or standards that are identified as learning outcomes for students in the various grades. Children are not immune to the emotional effects of this focus on their intellectual development because they sense the pressure adults are feeling.

This pressure is not inconsequential. In fact, our society imposes a great deal of pressure on children to succeed intellectually: it is promoted as the most important key to future success. As a consequence of this expectation, a child's self-esteem is closely associated with academic success. For the child, this pressure for academic success has considerable impact on self-esteem. Expressions such as "success breeds success" and "self-fulfilled prophecy" are not simply clichés: they have meaning and import for children in classrooms, and both are tied to the issue of relative-age effect and annual single-date entry.

Early success breeds confidence in a child, who will then feel able to attempt the learning challenges set out in a curriculum that is generally designed to have most students succeed. On the other hand, lack of success leads to self-doubt and self-imposed fear about tackling any new learning when failure seems probable. "I can't do this" soon becomes the student's mantra, leading to negative thought patterns of self-doubt and inadequacy, especially in relationship to peers.

The emotional well-being of a child is absolutely critical, because only one in eight grade-one students who fall behind the peer group are able to catch up later (Juel, 2003). Therefore, success in grade one is so critical for the child's well-being that rule makers in our society must consider all options which have the promise of improving a child's rate of success. If, as educators and politicians are so fond of saying, "Children are our country's most valuable resource," are we really doing all we can to accommodate the nurturing of this resource?

Unfortunately, the answer is, "No!" As already stated, a year to a grade one student represents 16 percent of their very brief lifetime. Substantial variances in intellectual development are readily apparent when two children sit in a classroom next to each other and the progress of one learner, who has lived approximately eighty months, is compared with another who has lived only sixty-eight months.

The school establishment will rise in righteous indignation at any suggestion that schools are competitive environments where students are compared to each other. Curriculum is written in such a way as to describe educational progress in terms of standards, not rank in a class. The child, however, does not understand this subtlety, nor do many parents. The child merely notices that their progress and success is not yet at the same level as others in the classroom. The result is negative self-esteem even though they are pursuing a standard. The parent, too, notices that a number of their child's peers have skills that their child does not have.

In grade one, the ability to read is an easily quantified skill that reflects individual progress. Teachers trained to assess students on a standard still find it "natural" and intuitive to compare students when differences are so apparent. Some teachers still "mark on the curve" where achievement relative to curricular standards is replaced with a focus on achievement relative to others in the class. Fortunately the number of teachers using this assessment technique is decreasing as more school systems adopt curriculum standards.

The central issue here is that some of the variance in early student achievement is merely a representation of a child's maturity based on their birth date. If this variance is significant to the extent that lives are impacted by loss of self-esteem and confidence, the cause of the variance must be considered for reform. However, the impetus for such reform must demonstrate a compelling story based on intelligence rather than merely intuition or anecdotal evidence.

In a recent discussion with a faculty of education, a professor noted that the issue of relative-age effect was not new and had been the topic of discussion in the university for some time. According to her, what was different now was that someone was finally bringing empirical evidence to the discussion. What had been anecdotal for many years was substantiated by a large database and a representative sample which permits extrapolation to the population as a whole. Previously small, isolated studies inhibited generalizations to all our students and schools.

The data record which follows in subsequent chapters permits a correlation study between relative-age effect and a student's success in learning. While others have addressed this topic, none have investigated the impact of the annual, single-date entry and its connection to achievement. It is the presence of both the relative-age effect and single-date entry that create an unfair and deleterious climate for many students.

The key points made in this chapter are:

- The annual single-date entry system has remained part of the education system's set of rules for generations.
- To a six-year-old child, one year is a monumental period of time because it represents approximately 16 percent of his or her life.
- Teachers, parents, and students all feel a pressure for the student to experience immediate success upon entering formal learning.
- A child's self-esteem is closely associated with academic success.
- A central issue is that some of the variance in early student achievement is merely a representation of a child's maturity based on his or her birth date.
- Schools have operated the same way for decades, but now empirical evidence is informing discussions on relative-age effect.

5

A Critical
Decision Moment

THE BEST APPROACH IS UNKNOWN

There are many moments of decision in the complex decision-making process which gives direction to our education system. Not all of these decision moments have significant impact on student success, but others are critical. This creates a serious challenge because the urgent and critical are not always one and the same, and both are commingled with a host of other decisions to create a situation which makes it difficult for educators and the public to thoughtfully and deliberately chart the best course of action. Consequently, many decisions are routinized, and parents simply defer to educators in the hope that they will make the best decision based on their experience and training.

This trust is warranted, partly because years of experience and ongoing training leave teachers well positioned to make prudential decisions. Furthermore, most accept the need for public accountability, even if there is some ambivalence and reluctance. In the case of single-date entry and the idea of a twelve-month cohort, many teachers recognize that old patterns and practices must be changed even if it involves altering accepted patterns of decision making.

However, change will need to start with others. Governments usually determine when children will begin attending school. Some latitude is usually granted to parents on the basis of information to which they are privy. For simplicity's sake, we will define entrance into the educational system as the time when a child is enrolled for formal learning, which is typically referred to as "grade one." Kindergarten and other school readiness programs, which prepare children for formal learning, operate in most parts of the world, but we are arbitrarily excluding them from this study even though there is no hard and fast line separating formal schooling from preschooling.

An examination of the rules governing entry into formal learning indicates considerable variation. Many school jurisdictions group children into birthday-based age cohorts that follow the traditional calendar year of January to December. These traditional schools typically start school around the beginning of September following an extended summer vacation.

There are simple variations to this approach, including one popular option which modifies the calendar so that children begin grade one at a slightly older age. In order to do this they require the sixth birthday to occur between October 1 and the following September 30. In this example, first-year students are potentially three months older than in the first model.

The United Kingdom provides an illustration of another approach within the parameters of the traditional model. In this case, the governing authorities require that a child's birthday fall between September 1 and the following August 31. This ensures that all children are six years of age before beginning grade one in September. Some countries in the Baltic region of northern Europe modify the entry year in the other direction, requiring that parents wait until age seven to enroll a child. By way of contrast, New Zealand enrolls children in grade one on the first day of their birth month, whenever that may be in the calendar.

These alternative approaches to year-one enrollment indicate how educators recognize that the factors of age and the date of enrollment into formal education are both critical and that a good solution has yet to be universally agreed upon. What is not properly recognized is that an age difference of one-sixth of a child's life is critically related to a child's success in school and beyond.

The School and Home Partnership

So much of what happens in our lives is determined by how well we learn in school. Success in school is not simply a matter of doing well enough to pass a grade, but it also depends upon how successfully a grade is passed. There are milestone moments in a student's career when futures are determined, and decisions made are usually predicated on the degree of success achieved while progressing through the grades.

One of these milestones, and arguably the most notable of them, is the moment when a student is at the threshold of moving into senior high school. At this point the student is confronted with a series of alternatives or pathways leading to different career and college options. School grades earned in the year prior to the milestone moment are frequently utilized as the significant screen whereby future pathways are determined. For example, students may be faced with a criterion such as a 65 percent mark in a course to qualify for acceptance into a high school mathematics program leading to university acceptance.

Viewed this way, the milestones a child passes in school are really signposts to future success. There needs to be a pattern of success beginning in grade one that feeds and facilitates future successes along the way, and it begins in grade one. There are many other nonschool factors which impact success, but the ones the school has influence over are powerful and long-lasting. For this reason, a great deal of justified attention is now being given to the quality of school experience a child receives in a particular school and in a particular classroom. Perhaps the most notable attention is school accountability based on student test scores.

The more scrutiny society brings to bear on the educational experience, the clearer it becomes that aspects of the home life are similarly critical. Success is a both/and scenario. Instead of seeing themselves in a partnership for the well-being of the child, however, parents frequently enter into a "blame game" with the educational system in which they blame the educators and the school environment for their child's lack of success; in turn the educators blame the child's parents and home environment.

Both environments contribute to a student's educational success and, therefore, both can and should be the focus of reform. The critical issue is that both the home and school environments are dynamic and display a wide range of effectiveness.

At one end of the scale, there is the stereotypical home which is understood to be disadvantaged. By this it is usually meant that the occupants are renters, the mother and father are poorly educated and likely living apart, and the neighborhood has a high crime rate. While these characteristics of a disadvantaged home environment do exist and are highly correlated with failure in school, the relationship between parent and child can overcome many of the negative aspects found in such an environment, so that the child can rise above the stereotypical expectations.

Similarly schools that are typically classified as disadvantaged on a series of economic indicators from the community's catchment area may nevertheless be effective. School boards typically support such schools with social programs designed to compensate for inequalities. This is why breakfast and/or lunch programs now are available in many schools. Also, schools serving in low socioeconomic environments may receive additional compensatory staff to assist in dealing with low rates of student success.

In other words, low socioeconomic indicators do not condemn a school to failure, nor do they accurately depict intelligence or academic potential. What the indicators do is obscure many of the compensatory and beneficial things a school does to foster success. Attempts to assess service are quickly challenged and redirected by powerful stakeholder organizations whose agenda is best served by a focus on the socioeconomic status of the clientele. These interest groups even challenge the use of objective measurement instruments, such as standardized tests, for self-serving purposes.

ACCOUNTABILITY GAINS MOMENTUM

Issues such as these interfere with reform-oriented processes and make it difficult to have a productive discussion between the school and home. Nevertheless, in spite of misunderstandings, disagreements, and competing agendas, educators are often able to focus on student achievement and remain optimistic about a vision to see students achieve to their maximum potential.

Translating these ideas into measurable objectives for which they can be held accountable has proven to be a challenging but rewarding endeavor. Measuring individual potential is fraught with difficulty and, therefore, any attempt to hold accountable those associated with the education system and charged with the task of pursuing this vision is easily foiled.

Decades ago schools frequently embraced vision statements that incorporated the notion of maximizing human potential. At that time, identifying such a vision was acceptable because there was a paucity of accountability measures on which to assess student progress in learning, as well as a culture that did not emphasize accountability for services rendered. Words in such vision statements are appealing because they align with our society's sense of fairness and optimism while simultaneously remaining vague enough to avoid unpleasant assessment and readily determined outcomes.

Today, however, the landscape has changed dramatically in education, and it is expected that education, like business, should be able to produce a "bottom line"—a measurement that confirms a degree of goal achievement. Notwithstanding the fact that some stakeholders in the education system dispute the contention that we are able to accurately measure student achievement, assessment practices are now sufficiently sophisticated to permit a high degree of accuracy on a range of measurements.

This is particularly true of system-wide assessment, which is now more consistent and arguably more accurate than what occurs in a classroom, if the focus is on the standards and outcomes mandated by the curriculum. There are teachers who are very proficient in knowing grade level standards and assessing student work against mandated standards, but the variance in teacher marks remains considerable and open to challenge.

All of these assessment matters have a bearing on the relative-age-effect issue. It is tempting to merely isolate data related to a student's level of achievement by birth month. In a later chapter we will explore in greater detail difficulties associated with assessment, and in particular, with an approach that merely isolates data related to a student's level of achievement by birth month. Subjectivity is a major problem in the classroom. Teachers are human and subject to various forms of bias while performing their assessment responsibilities. Acknowledging this issue and its impact on educational practices, including relative-age effect, is one of the distinguishing goals of this book.

A STRATEGY FOR SCHOOLS

Even though there are significant variances in the talent of teachers across the system, most are striving to have their students succeed because teaching remains a vocation for them, rather than a job with a salary and agreeable working conditions. They enjoy seeing students grow and mature in holistic and positive ways.

For this reason, parents continue to turn to teachers for input and advice related to their child, and one of the first times they do this is when social convention tells them it is time for their child to be enrolled in grade one. Therefore, it is critical that teachers, and not just school boards and state governments, understand the critical role birth month plays, if there is only one annual single-date entry into the education system.

My personal experience with the long-term negative effects of this phenomenon is based on many years of work as a school administrator. During these years, quarterly reviews were conducted with every teacher in the school in which we discussed the success of every individual student in the school. We focused these reviews on many aspects of a student's progress including academic achievement in language arts and mathematics, as well as social development, work and study habits, and achievement on standardized assessments.

The primary motivating force behind these quarterly reviews was our personal desires to see each student in the school succeed in accordance with his or her capacity. It was a motivational vision shared with teachers and staff. This led us to look at specific interventions which might be necessary for a particular student and what information we needed from parents. Recording student progress by tracking a student's current grade level achievement in language arts and mathematics was a significant element in the review, and it served as a check and balance on how we were meeting each student's needs in the core areas of the curriculum.

Repeatedly teachers identified this progress review process, with its focus on the individual student, as the single most important educational activity undertaken by the school's administration. The comprehensive nature of this activity, supported by detailed notes on the proceedings, was classic action-research. Details in these records were most useful in monitoring yearly progress and the success of various interventions undertaken at the school.

The detailed information in the records also provided accountabilities for parents because the school's administrators could readily reference what the teacher had actually stated whenever the parent was, in some future discussion, indicating that we had not made them aware of their child's lack of progress. The ultimate objective was to provide parents with a summary of their child's progress relative to the learning outcomes envisioned in the curriculum and then to make decisions on interventions that would improve the chance of success for their child.

Parents consistently expressed their appreciation for the school's openness and honesty in reporting the specific grade level achievement demonstrated by their child. On too many occasions parents volunteered that schools their child had previously attended had not informed them that their child was experiencing difficulties to the point that their instructional level was well below that of age-level peers.

Ultimately the value of such a time-consuming process had to be measured relative to its impact on student achievement. The evidence for that impact culminated one day when the superintendent called the school office with a request to visit the school and "investigate" why students were demonstrating such high levels of student achievement and still improving. While the school community was in one of the poorest areas in the city (e.g., requiring installation of phone booths to compensate for the lack of this basic necessity in the home), standardized test results were far above expectation.

When the superintendent asked the teachers to explain the cause of their success, they spoke unequivocally and with one voice about the decisive role played by the grade level achievement process. All affirmed that the time-consuming effort made by the principal to meet quarterly with them to strategize about individual children was a key to student success and well worth the effort that was required.

While the process was judged to be beneficial for improving student success, it also led to a much clearer understanding of the factors which were contributing to student success in the school. Even more importantly, the process gave us insight into why many students failed to achieve their potential. Inevitably the process focused on the moral imperative of helping weak students achieve grade level expectations so that they could progress with age-level peers.

During the many years that this process was followed, birth month of the child, or the relative-age effect as it is also labeled, emerged as a critical determinant to success. So consistent was the direct relationship between birth month and school-based learning challenges that we frequently spoke to parents of the importance of knowing the "right" month for getting pregnant, and we referenced this as the most important "parenting skill" they needed to acquire. Of course parents saw the humor in this, but they also confirmed the veracity of the underlying principle when they spontaneously offered anecdotal evidence that older children in a grade level peer group were advantaged.

As it is with most conclusions researchers come to in the field of education, the harmful impact of the relative-age effect is not an absolute rule but a generalization. There are always going to be exceptions because children are born with significant variances in intellectual capacity. What is important to parents when they come to a significant decision point, such as enrolling their child into grade one, is that there is a generalization regarding relative-age effect which must be considered. In fact, it must be considered carefully and with great concern: evidence now exists that the date of enrollment into the system is one of the most important decisions parents will make about the future success of their child.

What was unknown in the past were the long-term consequences. The typical consequences are undeniable in the elementary school years, but does it persist into the high school years? Even more significantly, how pervasive is the effect on the student who pursues postsecondary education?

Using Only One Rule Introduces Unfairness

Surely the education system's rule makers can bring about a structural change that provides greater flexibility in the way students progress through the school system. It seems very unfair that so many students should be disadvantaged, as will be described in subsequent chapters, simply because parents did not have sufficient information to make an informed decision about the date of their enrollment in school.

Teachers participating in focus groups indicated that parents expressed feeling enormous social pressure to register their children in school even when they believed their child was not ready. This social pressure, created by the expectations of significant friends and relatives, was something they found difficult to resist. Only a knowledgeable, well-informed parent is likely to be sufficiently motivated to resist the pressure to conform.

School administrators indicated a particularly disturbing factor when parents were making the decision to register. Economic pressure now combines with social pressure to make it almost impossible for the uninformed parent to make a decision about the date of enrollment without proper consideration for the child's readiness. Custodial care for children while the parent is at work is affordable when the child attends school. Furthermore, if there is any doubt about what is best for the child and the parent, there is the comforting belief that the school will make all the changes necessary to accommodate the unique needs of the child.

Parents are not the only ones feeling pressure: teachers in the New York controversy indicate feeling a similar pressure. Grade one teachers sense a pressure early in the year to develop literacy and numeracy skills in their students. One teacher said, "The job of the kindergarten teacher is to get them to the emergent stage before grade one. If they are not, it can make the entire reading process very painful for them and turn them off very quickly." This comment implies that the starting gun for formal learning goes off when the student enters grade one because teachers feel the pressure from everyone to get their students reading.

With so many pressures converging at the critical moment of decision and with the stakes so high for the child's future success, it is imperative that decision makers be as informed as possible when it comes time for enrollment. Currently decisions are predicated too much on the adults' emotions and circumstances.

A decision of when to have a child enter formal education in an annual single-date-entry program can be the most important decision for many of our nation's most valuable resource. Even when the child is sufficiently mature, a parental decision to enroll a child who is not mature can have a serious negative effect on the child, and on the more mature peer group that is required to cope with the slow child's lack of progress.

The key points made in this chapter are:

- Many decisions are routinized, and parents simply defer to educators in the hope that they will make the best decision based on their experience and training.
- A number of alternative approaches to year-one enrollment evident in the world indicate how educators recognize that the factors of age and the date of enrollment into formal education are both critical and that a good solution has yet to be universally agreed upon.
- Low socioeconomic indicators do not condemn a child to failure, nor do they accurately depict intelligence or academic potential.
- Assessment practices are now sufficiently sophisticated to permit a high degree of accuracy on a range of measurements.
- Teachers are human and subject to various forms of bias while performing their assessment responsibilities.
- Many students fail to achieve their potential because of their birth month.
- In education, the harmful impact of the relative-age effect is not an absolute rule but a generalization.

6

It Is What It Isn't

TEACHERS' ASSESSMENTS ARE PROBLEMATIC

Frequently in education one issue has a ripple effect, leading to other issues. Relative-age effect is about students being significantly disadvantaged for factors beyond their control. In the background lurks another issue which we need to expose and address. In this case, it is the role that informed educators have in stonewalling change by responding to criticism in a defensive manner or by creating a negative backlash to research that is critical of some aspect of their work.

Our culture has adopted the phrase, "it is what it is." It reflects a fatalistic acquiescence to an existing reality which one assumes to be irrevocable. It is the attitude society has adopted to the issue of learning difficulties attributable to relative-age effect: it is what it is. The system is in place, it seems to serve society quite well, and we should leave "good enough alone." The fact is, however, that the appearance that "all is well," or at least as good as we can get it without a massive increase in spending, is false.

It is not what it appears to be. Change can be made that is cost effective and much better for society and millions of individual children. But to address the big issue of relative-age effect, the education establishment must first address one of the major underlying subissues that contribute to the problem, namely teachers' resistance to research related to assessment practices.

It is a recognized fact that assessment of student achievement is skewed. This, in itself, is not alarming, as an unbiased process would see the skewing develop in multiple directions so that negative and positive results cancel each other out. But this is not the case. The assessment of students' work is inflated to such a degree that it distorts student progress. In other words, the teachers' actual conviction of a student's achievement is not reported to parents or the public. As a consequence, the relative-age effect is even more significant than if there was a high level of consistency in how teachers interpreted student achievement.

The large, longitudinal study which informs much of this book begins with data collected in grade three. This is the first year that students write a standardized test in language arts and mathematics. All students are expected to write these tests, but the superintendent may exempt a child if he or she determines that the test is beyond a student's intellectual capacity and may result in personal frustration leading to loss of self-esteem. Historically, more than 90 percent of grade three students write these tests, which are generally given in the penultimate week of the school year.

Student achievement is publicly reported according to two standards. The Acceptable Standard is approximately equivalent to a passing mark of 50 percent, and the Standard of Excellence is achieved at approximately the 80 percent level or a grade of A. While parents and schools receive an individual student profile recording the student's actual score on each component of the tests, system reporting is based on the percentage of students achieving these two standards. The Acceptable Standard includes the percentage of students who achieved the Standard of Excellence because these students also demonstrated learning at the Acceptable Standard.

A standards approach is intended to do away with the bell curve, which distributes scores according to a set formula. The goalposts are constantly moving in a bell curve environment; as a consequence, the curve represents a picture which is always shifting because specified percentages of students must fail, must receive an A, must receive a B, and so forth. In a standards approach, all students can be assessed at an A level, and all can be assessed as having failed. The standard is set and does not vary relative to class or group performance.

This means it does not compare students with each other but with a curriculum standard. The goalposts remain fixed from one administration of the test to another and from one group of students to another, as well as from one year to another. When standards are used, parents and the public can be more certain that student marks will be consistent across a system without nonacademic biases being applied.

A critical understanding of measurement issues is that these tests are equated to previous years so that test results may be compared over time. This procedure is seldom understood by the public, which frequently assumes that tests are automatically at the same level of difficulty when, in fact, they are not. Making tests equal in difficulty requires a great deal of work and experience, and it remains an ongoing concern with standardized testing.

It is also important to understand that classroom teachers do not have the training, resources, or time to equate their assessment instruments or undertake reliability and validity checks. This is a significant factor in helping people understand why summative assessments produced by teachers for their own classrooms are considerably less reliable than standardized assessments prepared for system-wide use.

Given the challenges that test makers have in producing a test that measures what it purports to measure over time, it is troubling that teachers receive so little training in assessment. Surveys of new teachers indicate they are more dissatisfied with their training in this area than in any other. This failure on the part of our universities' faculties of education is hard to understand given the essential role assessment plays in revealing what, when, and how something needs to be taught. Assessment is foundational for good teaching, and awareness of its importance has increased. A review of topics at current educator conferences reveals that seminars on assessment are a "hot topic."

Parents generally are unaware of the lack of preparation teachers have in assessment, and that different teachers may vary greatly in their assessment of a particular piece of work. Inconsistent assessment by classroom teachers is one aspect of the problem. Grade inflation is another, as students from K–12 and the postsecondary level are frequently given credit for higher levels of achievement than they actually demonstrated.

A well-constructed standardized test designed by a professional test maker requires hundreds of hours of work. It includes in-depth consultation with classroom teachers to write good questions, and it involves a field testing of each question. This extensive effort results in a test that provides a more accurate depiction of student achievement on a specified curricular standard than a routine test created by a classroom teacher.

Standardized, system-wide tests that make use of questions that can be scored by a machine are often referred to as "multiple choice." Constructing a good multiple choice question is a sophisticated science. Some stakeholders in the education system attempt to belittle the achievement by renaming multiple choice tests as multiple "guess" tests. Virtually every reader will have experienced this type of question and understand that guessing may be part of a valid approach.

Some people may believe that they can actually guess the right answers a sufficient number of times to achieve a passing mark. Using thoughtful guesses to obtain a few marks and a passing grade is feasible, but one experiment showed that a student who guessed on all the questions of a scientifically prepared multiple choice test had a probability of passing of one in one billion. That is, it would normally take fifty thousand students over a period of twenty-thousand years for someone to have guessed enough right answers to achieve a passing score.

In comparison, there is a much greater likelihood of being hit by lightning twice in a lifetime. Lottery participants frequently face far better odds at winning with some lotteries offering millions of dollars where the probability of winning is one in fourteen million (not billion) chances. Random guessing on a well-constructed multiple choice test would leave a student with virtually no chance of passing.

Some tests also utilize constructed response components which require students to provide a written answer to questions. Written responses are more subjective because marker bias and interpretation are involved. For example, studies have found significant levels of gender bias when teachers mark student work. Also, there are biases related to the socioeconomic status of the family as well as biases related to cultural origin and a student's program distinction (e.g., enrollment in an English as a Second Language program).

Teacher Biases Lead to Inconsistent Assessment

One study (Webber et al., 2009) found that approximately 60 percent of teachers are influenced by the student's background when assessing student work. Teachers adjusted marks according to the characteristics of the student's home environment and whether or not the student was from an immigrant family. A complete listing and explanation of biases is unnecessary because the point is that they exist, that they are not going away, and that the school system must have ways to correct the misinformation that results.

The simple fact of knowing that the student and the teacher are acquainted creates an opportunity for teachers to knowingly or unknowingly develop a marking bias. The written component of a test used in the assessment of student learning should always be marked by at least two teachers, preferably one of whom has no knowledge of the writer. Seldom is this the case in classroom tests! Overwhelmingly classroom teachers utilize only one reader, and that reader knows the person writing very well.

In the system examination program in this study, the student's teacher could undertake the first of two readings. When they did, the classroom teacher invariably read more into the answer than the response warranted. The teacher's thought process seems to have been that since they had taught this student a specific concept, they must actually know it better than the student had demonstrated in the answer written on the test paper. Grade inflation is an obvious result.

In this study, the written response for the system test was marked by at least two teachers. When the mark varied by more than 20 percent, we used a third marker. These tests were low stakes, by which we mean the level of the funding for the child was not put at risk by the test results, and grade promotion for the student also was not at stake. This made it particularly reasonable for the student's teacher to be one of the test readers, and almost 70 percent undertook this marking activity before sending it to the test-marking center for anonymous marking.

The marking center was staffed by teachers who received extensive training before beginning the marking process. We expected this training to help the markers interpret the standards as they were intended to be interpreted and with consistency. Not only did the markers not know the students' identity, but they did not know in which geographic region of the school system the students resided. These factors taken together enabled us to compare the interpretations of teachers who knew the students to those who did not know them.

The results revealed a substantial difference between the scores of the two test groups. Over a five-year period, grade three teachers who knew their students gave 85 percent more of them a mark in the Standard of Excellence range than did teachers who were part of the system's centralized marking program, but who did not know the students. In other words, 85 percent more grade three students received an A from their teacher than from an anonymous teacher.

In grade six during the five-year period, 110 percent more students received a mark in the Standard of Excellence range from their own teacher and, in grade nine, the difference was 63 percent. Clearly, biases toward grade inflation were evident when the teacher knew the student even though the student would never know whether or not the teacher had marked their particular test. The other interesting and disturbing point to be made from this data is that the tendency to grade inflation was most pronounced with students at the upper end of the spectrum. In other words, the likelihood of grade inflation on the part of the classroom teacher increased as the marks became higher.

The problem of grade inflation in the classroom was not significantly reduced even after bringing this concern to the attention of school districts. In the next five-year period, the number of grade three students who received an inflated mark from their classroom teacher declined from 85 percent to 74 percent, but in grade six it increased to 118 percent. The decline for students in grade nine was from 63 percent to 45 percent.

In spite of this compelling data gathered over a ten-year period, the school system was unwilling to implement viable strategies to help classroom teachers address this serious problem. Even discussions about making teachers and parents aware of the classroom teacher's propensity toward grade inflation were viewed by trustees and administrators as threatening and explosive. Consequently, they chose to keep the information confidential.

The tendency for grade inflation was also evident at the Acceptable Standard or pass/fail threshold. Overall, approximately 10 percent of students who failed to achieve the Acceptable Standard from the anonymous, marking-center teacher received a passing mark from their own teacher. Given the similarity of scores in this range, it appears that assessing minimal competency is easier to master or that bias is less likely when teachers are simply scoring "acceptability."

The story of grade inflation in this longitudinal study is one that has been told often in the literature. This decade-long study reveals yet again the tendency for teachers who know a student to allow factors to influence their assessment of a student's work. In all likelihood, the influence is subliminal rather than intentional, and is usually the result of students exhibiting compliance—cooperative behavior, good attendance, completed homework, and in-class participation—which is being factored into assessments of students' work. These compliant aspects are desirable, but they should not influence an assessment of a student's ability to answer a particular question.

The consistency of these findings over many years in such a large-scale testing program in a school system with more than six hundred thousand students supports the well-documented conclusions that teachers are prone to inflate marks and that the tendency for grade inflation increases at higher levels of student achievement. Therefore, parents and students benefit from knowing their achievement on standardized tests, and the general public is able to utilize this large-scale testing program as an accountability tool for assessing performance by the teacher, school, school district, and school system.

The public is usually astonished to see the difference between marks a student receives from their own teacher and the mark he or she receives from an anonymous teacher when assessing the same piece of student work. Generally they are oblivious to the reality of grade inflation because they are only focused on their child. They do not see large-scale data which exposes the degree to which a tendency is evident across an entire school system. When they see the complete picture, they are amazed by the degree and typically become supporters of large-scale testing using anonymous marking strategies.

Educators in the system are also astonished by the information and perplexed about what can and should be done to ameliorate the problem. One metropolitan school district superintendent indicated that grade inflation was actually pandemic within his school district. Of course he was referencing the existence of tendencies for grade inflation involving his entire teaching force, which included many teachers who did not even participate in centralized marking activities where rigorous training takes place.

Some teachers in grades three, six, and nine do not undertake the first marking. Also, teachers for grades one, two, four, five, seven, and eight never have the opportunity to participate in centralized marking. These teachers, who were not involved in ongoing assessment in-service—such as a marking center—where their marks were compared with peers, were likely to experience far more significant differences than those participating in the centralized marking process.

This prompted the superintendent involved in this study to operate a program utilizing centralized marking where anonymity was ensured. His school district also conducted district-wide tests in addition to the regional testing program. Every summer teachers would mark tests that would also be marked by others. Participating in this additional centralized marking activity provided these teachers with an opportunity to compare their interpretations of student responses relative to curriculum standards. Unfortunately, it did not become a widespread practice in this region or, for that matter, across the education system.

This region's testing program also provided evidence of what happens when teachers' marks on the same piece of student work were compared after the markers had the benefit of concentrated in-service immediately prior to the marking exercise. It is logical to expect considerable consistency after concentrated coaching on how to mark specific responses on the examination, especially when the assessment was high stakes for the student, such as exists for a student sitting for a grade twelve diploma examination. In this longitudinal study, not only was there intensive training prior to commencing actual marking but markers received daily feedback once the marking session was under way.

Whenever the mark on an examination question varied by more than 20 percent between the two markers, a third reader was utilized to provide greater accuracy. In English, fully one in four papers required a third reader. In other words, 25 percent of test answers were marked with a score that varied between the two markers by more than 20 percent. In science courses, third-reader rates were considerably less at approximately 4 percent because the answers were more objective: students could obtain credit by merely providing a few words or short sentences.

This data involved teachers who received intensive training prior to the marking activity. They also benefited from ongoing feedback once the marking process began. Despite all of this effort at trying to ensure high levels of consistency, the difference between teachers' perceptions of student responses on the tests is disturbing. These differences are especially pronounced in the humanities, including specifically English and social studies, where student answers are lengthy. Since most teachers do not participate in such ongoing professional development in marking as that which occurs in the regional marking activities, the potential for inconsistent assessments increases.

Grade Inflation Is a Natural but Fraudulent Tendency

The significance of the grade inflation phenomenon will become very evident in a subsequent chapter. The point here is to establish the fact of the problem and then to describe the extent: it is not an irrelevant, anomalous statistic associated with some faraway education system. A review of the educational literature reveals that it is a worldwide concern. In fact, to deal with the scope and impact of this problem would require a book. What follows is a short synopsis of the problem.

Michael Woods (2008), references a study by James Coté which describes the problem as it exists in Ontario, Canada. In 2008, 90 percent of Ontario's grade twelve students graduated with a B or A average, with 60 percent applying for university entrance having an A average. The report concludes that "The number of 'A' students isn't growing because people are getting smarter. Rather, academic standards have declined so it is easier to get an 'A' than ever before—a phenomenon known as grade inflation."

The report goes on to summarize the historic trend of an ever-increasing percentage of Ontario students registering for university with an A average. In 1983, only 15 percent of students registered for university with an A average from their school. By 2004 that percentage had increased to 25 percent and by 2007 to 40 percent. It is important to understand that Ontario does not make use of an exit exam at the end of grade twelve. Therefore final marks submitted to postsecondary institutions are the assessments provided by classroom teachers only. There is no check and balance system holding educators accountable for marks being given in the classroom.

Within a span of twenty-four years, the percentage of students receiving an A average in grade twelve almost tripled; yet in 2009 Ontario's instructors of first-year students were requested to complete a survey regarding that province's student preparedness for university. Only 2 percent of these instructors perceived an improvement in student preparedness for university, while the majority indicated "less preparedness."

Coincidentally, another Canadian province, Alberta, reported a similar finding in their 2009 survey of postsecondary instructors across the province. Not only was student readiness a significant concern in every discipline but student writing skills were found to be particularly weak with only a 20 percent satisfaction rating. Alberta's grade twelve graduates were also asked regarding their writing skills, with 87 percent of students indicating a perception that they had the necessary skills for postsecondary education. A difference of 67 percent between instructors and students demonstrates how far below expectations grade twelve graduates really were. This information is disturbing because it is obvious that students are very misled regarding their readiness for the next level of education.

Grade inflation has also been a national problem for the United States. Recently the federal Department of Education launched its Race to the Top initiative where the K–12 school system is obligated to improve student learning so that postsecondary institutions are certain that new students entering that system have the requisite knowledge and skills. The initiative also requires postsecondary institutions to abandon their costly, long-standing use of remedial courses deemed necessary to compensate for the inadequate preparation of freshmen for college and university.

Thomas and Bainbridge (1997) studied many school districts across the United States, and they came to the same conclusion as those studying the problem in Canada. To illustrate the pattern they saw, they reported on one school district whose students received the highest grade point averages at 3.6 but whose SAT scores were the lowest in the school board's jurisdiction. On the other hand, a different school had the lowest grade point average (2.5) but the highest test scores of the schools.

So frequently did they discern a similar pattern across American school districts that they actually labeled the phenomena a "fraudulent practice," concluding that:

> In low achieving schools with high grade point averages, expectations are extremely low—just the opposite of what research indicates should be done. Having low expectations begets low achievement. The fraud is that the high grade point average gives a false message to the students. Schools which expect little and provide high grades, regardless of the level of academic achievement, are fraudulent educational systems and should be corrected.

A natural response to this data could be, "So what; who cares?" Some will suggest that giving students higher marks than they deserve helps their self-esteem. Yet studies about grade inflation find that as grade inflation increases, student achievement on standardized tests actually decreases (Laurie, 2007). Therefore, inflated marks actually serve to demotivate students by lulling them into a false sense of success in their achievement.

If students experience a false sense of security, parents, too, are lulled into believing that everything is fine. Furthermore, the public has no evidence that a problem exists, no "red flag" alerting activities of the need for corrective action. Once again, there is a general hands-off passivism that assumes, "it is what it is," when in fact it is not what it appears to be: achievement is below standard and far below the excellent scores awarded by the students' teachers. Without external pressure brought to bear on the issue, the educational system remains complacent.

Inaccurate teacher assessments of students' work are best explained by a lack of professional training, not proper motivation or malpractice. A study (Webber et al.) of the literature around the world conducted in 2009 concluded that "Reporting to stakeholders clearly, accurately, and sensitively is among the most difficult and uncomfortable parts of student evaluation for teachers and, therefore, may result in student achievement not being reliably conducted, interpreted, or reported."

Webber et al. point out that everywhere educators are finding how difficult it is for teachers to report to stakeholders. It is a task that should only be undertaken by those who have been thoroughly and appropriately trained. They also offer an additional observation: those providing assessment are uncomfortable with the task, presumably because of the pressures inherent in the relationship between teachers and parents, teachers and students, and even parents and their children.

These twin problems of difficulty and discomfort lead to "soft evaluation strategies" that reduce teacher anxiety and foster a marking strategy that gives students the "benefit of the doubt." In other words, when faced with uncertainty and a lack of conviction or incontrovertible evidence, the benefit of doubt leads teachers to inflate the mark. It is easier to maintain positive relationships between the various participants when the news is good even though the news is inaccurate.

Grade Inflation Obscures the Problem

It is time now to draw back the veil of secrecy which has obscured the practice of grade inflation. In this book, the primary concern relates to the role this plays in the issue of relative-age effect, but its pernicious influence is felt in many other areas. By consistently overstating a student's success in the classroom, teachers suppress the seriousness of the situation that the system needs to address for the well-being of the student.

Relative-age effect negatively impacts many students in the school system, but the tendency of educators to inflate student success has the effect of reducing the real impact of the age spread. In other words, the operational rule which requires students twelve months apart in age to be bundled together in a single and supposedly homogenous cohort creates serious problems that impact a child for the rest of his or her life. Exacerbating this problem is that teachers have masked the seriousness by providing an overly optimistic assessment of their students' progress. This means that the data reported later in this book actually understates the problem related to relative-age effect.

If the ancillary problem of grade inflation did not exist, there might be more public awareness of the relative-age effect, and with this awareness would come more public attention and more calls for action. This is particularly true of the negative impact on the classroom of students born in the latter half of the year: their grades are particularly overstated, and the impact of their relatively poor performance on the more mature children born in the first half of the year underestimated and understated. Later, this book sets out the way in which talented students are unknown victims in a school system that is so focused on meeting the educational needs of weaker students.

This focus has been coined a "moral imperative" (Fullan, 2003) and summarizes how the education system places so much emphasis on ensuring that all students are successful. This is strong language which states in emphatic terms how committed our system is to seeing that all students are successful, even if the assessment creates illusion and distortion.

A problem is that teachers have so many students functioning below grade level that their classroom instruction may be too focused on these weak students require to achieve only a pass. What is success for students at the upper level of achievement? When some students—in this case the more able and mature—are not recipients of attention necessary to maintain their high levels of achievement, the moral imperative that envisions an obligation to help the less mature penalizes them for their ability and maturity. A grade inflation tendency at the upper level as indicated in this chapter has provided many students, and thus their parents, with false information regarding their ongoing success.

This information actually underscores another related, fundamental problem, namely that the bell curve philosophy of assessment continues to influence teachers. The bell curve subconsciously fosters grade inflation because students are rated against each other rather than against curricular criteria. A percentage of students are always rated as high achievers, but with today's competition for entry into postsecondary institutions, teachers feel a pressure to have their students qualify. Hence there is a propensity toward grade inflation.

For other teachers, it may be that the reporting is so uncomfortable that it is easier to report higher achievement than what is realistic. Being recognized as a bastion of high standards may be motivation for some teachers, but being an outlier may also leave one seen as a "sore thumb" requiring some corrective attention. It is not unusual for students to select teachers who are known to give higher marks.

One teacher related his experience regarding a three-hour period at the beginning of the school term when all the teachers sat in the gymnasium. Students lined up outside the school doors, and when they were open hundreds rushed to their "favorite" teachers to switch into his or her section. This left "duds" and those who graded "hard" with many students leaving their section for other popular, high fliers. It was described as a circus with a carnival atmosphere. Well intentioned, as usual, but demoralizing to many teachers.

The system wanted students to move to teachers with whom they could learn; "it" also wanted students to take electives they really wanted, which meant some courses had to be dropped. It all made sense, but there was a lot of winks and chuckles going on with teachers smirking behind the backs of their colleagues who only had students exiting their classes. Many teachers were bitter, embarrassed, depressed, and highly demotivated—or arrogant and quite determined to do what it took to keep receiving good strokes from the students. Was grade inflation a villain in this process? In this teacher's opinion, the answer was a resounding, "yes!"

Whatever the case, substantially fewer students are being assessed as having not met grade level expectations than is actually occurring, and the impact on the data regarding relative-age effect is diluted. If assessments on student achievement relative to learning outcomes were more closely aligned to curriculum standards, the data could conceivably bring more attention to the issue and provoke more public pressure for a system response.

Discussing relative-age effect would be much simpler and considerably less contentious if the issue of grade inflation was irrelevant. It is not. In fact, it seriously aggravates the situation and makes reform even more difficult because the educational establishment needs to address multiple, intersecting issues simultaneously. Even though governments are pursuing increased transparency, this information, once disseminated, could give the impression that the education system is not well and a self-serving cover-up is to blame.

An experience with one teachers' union revealed how badly they wanted this issue kept from public view. They formally requested that the department not permit the releasing of information to other stakeholders in the system and certainly not to the public. Why? Because the union believed the information would potentially adversely affect the public's confidence in the school system. The union's thrust was to avoid any disclosures that might create parental concern with educational services provided by their members.

Nevertheless, it is a story that must be told and a record of failure we must openly discuss and address. The trends evident currently in assessing student achievement are diluting other issues in education which would benefit from discussion where more accurate assessment was occurring. Relative-age effect is one issue which is not recognized adequately because of the propensity of the education system toward grade inflation. In other words, a "tipping point" might be more readily achieved because the current situation regarding student achievement as reported by classroom teachers is not what it is. What it isn't is a process of student evaluation that is consistent and accurate.

The key points made in this chapter are:

- The assessment of students' work is inflated to such a degree that it distorts student progress.
- Teachers' classroom assessments are considerably less reliable than standardized assessments prepared for system-wide use.
- Studies have found significant levels of gender bias when teachers mark student work.
- The likelihood of grade inflation on the part of the classroom teacher increased as the marks became higher.
- Inflated marks actually serve to demotivate students by lulling them into a false sense of success in their achievement.
- The tendency of educators to inflate student success has the effect of reducing the real impact of the age spread.
- If the problem of grade inflation did not exist, there might be more public awareness of the relative-age effect, and with this awareness would come more public attention and more calls for action.

7

Student Achievement by Birth Month

EVERY MONTH MAKES A DIFFERENCE

Data from an extensive study reveals the significance of the relative-age effect in an annual single-date entry system on student achievement (see figure 7.1). If it is true that a "picture is worth a thousand words," then this picture should be sufficient reason to challenge rule makers about continuing their current practices. The results of this carefully crafted and monitored study over a six-year period shows a steady drop in achievement in the April to December age groups. It provides incontrovertible evidence that the majority of students are not maximizing their learning potential in the current twelve-month cohort system.

The figure shows language arts test results by way of mean achievement scores for all students with a birthday in a particular month of the school year. Students born in March have the highest test scores, and results for subsequent months show a gradual, but statistically significant, decline. Simply stated, older students' achievement is higher than that of younger ones.

Whereas a small majority of school districts have a school registration cutoff date of December 31, many school districts extend the cutoff to the end of the second February. As the bar graph reaches the right side of the chart, the achievement level of students born in the second January and February fits the pattern that younger students achieve at lower levels than older students.

The test results for these second January and February birth-month students make apparent the foolishness of school districts permitting children born in these months to enroll in school when they are as young as five and one half years old. It is an unconscionable abuse of authority for leaders to admit groups of students into a class when it is known their chances of success are significantly reduced.

One of the interesting, consistent features of figure 7.1 is the success of students born in March. Based on the rest of the evidence, this is counterintuitive. Students born in March are not the oldest, but they demonstrate the highest level of achievement. January and February birth-month students are older but demonstrate a slightly lower level of achievement. The tragedy within this graphic is that there are many students who started school in their second January or February but were too immature to achieve success. They were subsequently retained for a year, and then wrote the grade three tests with the cohort of students born during the regular January to December registration period.

Even though these students spent an additional year in school and were now with their age cohort, their achievement on the test was not as high as that of their same-age peers who started school when they were six years old. In other words, the immature, retained learner pulled down the January and February results because the damage to their self-esteem mitigated some of

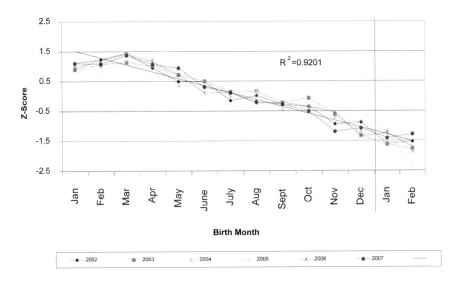

FIGURE 7.1.

the success they would have experienced had they waited to start school with their age cohort. In effect, the education system penalized these younger students.

Success in life is not about performance in a one-off event but about a pattern of positive experiences that leads to a holistic health and well-being. One of the essential building blocks for such a life is a child's grade one experience. In choosing to minimize the significance of this we are trifling with a principle that impacts children for the rest of their lives. When students wrote system tests in grade three, the age difference between students born in the first January and the second February was as great as fourteen months. Not surprisingly, many students born in the second January and February "fell off the bus" and ended up being retained at grade level.

This phenomenon will be discussed in more detail in subsequent chapters, but the impact on their success in school even after being retained is so significant that when they did write the system tests they actually brought down the first January and February achievement levels to below the success achieved by the March birth-month students. If all school districts followed the same rule and utilized December 31 as the cutoff, the graph on birth-month student achievement would have been the highest for January.

The data in figure 7.1 yields additional information of note. First, the phenomenon is consistent across several years and provides visual evidence that student achievement by grade three is related to birth month. Such measurement precision is powerful and requires a thoughtful response from the rule makers on whether our education system is really operating in the best interests of all students.

Second, the data demonstrates the precision of these system tests as an instrument for measuring student achievement. The mathematics tests resulted in the same pattern of correlations and the same trend line. This argues strongly for the reliability of these standardized tests, as they are able to assess analogous groups with analogous results. Those suspicious of standardized testing find it difficult to explain away the overwhelming consistency demonstrated by such instruments.

Data for fourth-year students but in grade three is not included in this short summary. However, it reveals that students in their fourth year who were born in the second January and February period were still unable to achieve at the same level as their birth-month peers, in spite of being held back one year. The difficulty which began in grade one continued to unfold; once they fell behind, they remained behind and experienced an ongoing penalty imposed upon them by the system, not because they were less able, but because they were younger.

As previously stated, change is difficult, especially when society has imposed a rule or convention for more than a century. Exposing a fallacy in the rule places considerable pressure on educational leaders, because ignoring the evidence really brings into question issues of motivation and conflict of interest.

Anecdotal explanations which administrators, teachers, and parents offered in discussions provided a plausible, if unconscionable, explanation for the existence of a second February 28 cutoff registration date. The intention of the decision makers was that a provision of an extended cutoff date would entice parents to register in their system, rather than another school district with an overlapping attendance boundary that had a December 31 cutoff date. School administrators in this study readily admitted that this policy, which about 50 percent of the school districts adopted, was based on financial considerations.

In most communities there were two publicly funded systems available which resulted in competition for enrollment. Many parents wanted their child to begin attending school as early as possible because of the no-cost, high-quality custodial care available in a regular school setting during the workday. The opportunity for free custodial care one year earlier than what was available with the other school district enticed some parents to select one district over the other. Convenience and economics were a higher priority than the child's best interests.

While school personnel are aware that intellectual development is a factor in student success, many parents lack the same degree of awareness. Furthermore, given the lack of a relevant database on student achievement related to age-based cohorts, parental decisions about enrollment were based on intuition and anecdotal evidence. Now that data is available, decision makers should make it known and address directly the unfair practice of enticing early registration for self-serving purposes.

Until proactive voices are heard and heeded, it is likely the practice will continue because district educational leaders generally believe that parents will continue to enroll their children in a school system that accommodates their desire for early enrollment. In other words, it is believed that "once in, always in" is the most likely result.

In summary, the analysis of achievement data by birth month reveals how rules disadvantage a significant percentage of our students. At this point, it is appropriate to reiterate the quip that an important aspect of parenting is knowing when to become pregnant. During a recent discussion of this issue with a group of parents, one mother responded to the provocative statement above by reminding everyone that "family planning" is an important aspect of cattle ranching.

While this was probably an attempt at humor, based on the idea that school boards should be at least as smart as cattle breeders, there is a sober philosophical point to be made: children are infinitely more valuable than cattle, so what are we doing creating obvious scenarios that lead to disadvantage and failure! It was as though she was saying, "This is something that we would never tolerate in any other realm of human endeavor, even the cattle industry."

Ranchers ensure that breeding is planned so that calves are not born in November when they have to survive hostile winters, but in the spring when they have several months to gain sufficient strength before the next winter season. "Family planning" is an important aspect of the beef industry. Indeed a drive through ranch country in the month of May reveals herds of cows, bison, and horses with huge numbers of very young offspring.

In the school context with a January to December registration period, effective family planning suggests pregnancy in June so that the child is born in March unless the parent is strong enough to resist the temptation to enroll their child in a district with an end of second-February cutoff. If the temptation can be overcome, then the best month for pregnancy is April for entry into the school system in January. A January birth month provides the typical North American child with significant advantage in two domains: the physical as demonstrated in Gladwell's book, and the intellectual.

In discussions with parent groups, reactions to this finding evoke interesting responses. Parents with children who were born in the first few months of the year beam with pride that they "did it right" and frequently react by giving "high-fives" with other parents of similar good fortune. Presumably they were merely the recipients of good fortune rather than the arbiters of good family planning.

One of the more interesting responses to this research came from a government bureaucrat who reviewed the birth-month data and said that it does not prove that older students achieve at higher levels than younger ones. His assertion was that students born in December simply may not be as intelligent as those born in January. After all, this could be a phenomenon similar to astrology's "signs of the zodiac," where people demonstrate characteristic variances depending on the time of year they were born.

This bureaucrat was frustrated by this relative-age-effect information because it had implications for leadership and, specifically, his leadership. Hopefully the observation was made in jest, but it was a challenge that required a thoughtful response because this research has not involved control groups. Therefore, like a crown prosecutor in a trial, circumstantial evidence had to be assembled to overcome his cynicism and guilt.

Fortunately such a case study was readily available with a school system utilizing a different rule for entry than the January to December calendar so typical in North America. The United Kingdom also has a history of testing at key stages of a student's educational career; however, their system utilizes a September to August birth calendar as opposed to January through December. Therefore children in the United Kingdom have the oldest students begin their schooling with a September birth month and the youngest with an August birth month.

Students write a Key Stage test at the age of seven or the conclusion of their second year in school; their pattern of achievement is depicted in figure 2 below. Given the robustness of the theory, it is not surprising that the pattern of achievement and maturity parallels those in this study. Each birth

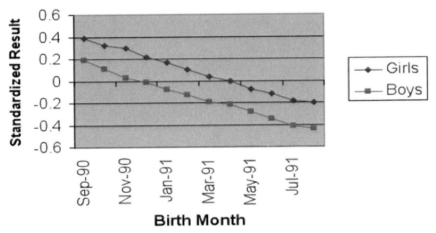

FIGURE 7.2.

month has lower levels of achievement for both genders than was evident in the preceding month. The data from the United Kingdom as well as the data from this study confirm patterns of student achievement by birth month. Children born in one specific month are not smarter than those born in another. Rather, those born earlier have greater intellectual maturity, which is precisely what one would suspect.

STANDARDIZED TESTS ARE AN UNWELCOME MESSENGER

Skeptics who discount the relative-age effect exist because the data utilized in these analyses are based on standardized test results. Some education stakeholders endeavor to persuade the public, including parents, that standardized tests are inaccurate measures of student achievement and should be avoided. This opposition is usually the result of increased accountability placed on educators where consequences, including pay for performance, are applied.

These voices fail to recognize that teachers constantly make use of standardized tests in their classrooms, because the working definition of a standardized test is any test given to two or more people. Classroom teachers constantly utilize spelling tests, quizzes, end of chapter and unit tests, commercially prepared tests, as well as tests they prepare on their own. To vilify system-wide, standardized tests is really a smokescreen to avoid efforts at accountability for student achievement.

Genuine skeptics of standardized testing frequently express their opposition to the administration of these tests to more than one class, school, or school district in order for student achievement to be assessed across a school, district, or region. In other words, it is the ability to provide comparative data concerning student achievement that creates anxieties for people in the education system who feel insecure.

Yet this type of information is what the public wants and needs to know. Parents want to know which teachers in their child's school have a talent for adding value to student achievement. Every educator impacts student achievement! The significant question is whether that impact is positive or negative? When standardized tests are given in many classrooms throughout a region, the answer to this question can be ascertained and the impact measured.

In an effort to address the concerns of reticent teachers and administrators, my region decided to institute a "balanced approach" to accountability. This meant that monitoring through standardized testing of grade level achievement for grades one to nine was supplemented with an assessment by the classroom teacher. The blend of objective classroom assessment with teacher observation, which was based in theory on all aspects of the curriculum, was laudable, but this approach to assessment includes moving standards which are idiosyncratic to each teacher. This makes comparison between individuals and groups problematic.

This is not simply because teachers are inconsistent in the way they apply standards, although this is a significant challenge in and of itself. The other problem arises from the fact that teachers bring varying philosophies into the assessment matrix. During a presentation in Atlanta, where there were about 2,000 educators in attendance, Robert Marzano presented ten marks for a course's assessment and then asked the audience to provide the final mark.

With everyone looking at the same information and applying their own perspectives, final marks ranged from A to F or 90 percent to 30 percent. Such a lack of consistency is customary because teachers, consciously or unconsciously, draw on their grading policy when they mark an assignment and compile results for a cumulative grade. The inconsistency occurs because educational systems too frequently delegate assessment policies to individual teachers.

For example, a teacher must decide how incomplete assignments should be scored, what to do with assignments that are submitted, and how to respond to suspected cheating. There is also the issue of weighted scores: should they give a greater value to tests at the end of the course, and how does one assess the relative value of daily assignments or written homework and in class tests? Then there are issues of neatness, precision, accuracy in spelling, stylistic features, and grammar—all of which are likely to vary from assignment to assignment, and certainly from teacher to teacher. These and similar questions are usually handled by individual teachers, and involve some philosophical grounding.

To reduce the extraneous and detracting effects of teacher inconsistency and philosophical orientation, the region's administration asked teachers to use a simpler system of assessment that looked at the grade level achievement of individual children. In doing this, we were able to get an assessment that tapped the same basic question the standardized tests investigated. Teachers were asked to indicate if a student was "at," "above," or "below" grade placement. Teachers applied their own perceptions regarding students' achievement relative to standards and applied their own interpretations of how the summative evaluation should be made.

An analysis of their work revealed that the teachers perceived a significant difference between students born earlier than later in the school year, even though the issue of age difference was not before them when they did their evaluation. In other words, they were unaware that we would be correlating their assessment with age. A much higher percentage of students born earlier in the year were rated "at" or "above" grade level when compared to students born later in the year.

Also, students born in January or February were scored lower in terms of their grade level achievement than March-born children. Once again, there is evidence of the deleterious effect of registering second January-February born children. This means that teacher assessment, corrected in essential ways to take into account inconsistencies and philosophies, and standardized tests both came to the same conclusion.

This research revealed one additional aspect of grade-based achievement by birth month. Figure 7.3 below depicts gender achievement in grade three language arts as measured by standardized tests. In all birth months, girls' achievement is higher than boys', which is not surprising because it is a well-established fact that girls do better in language arts. Normally we treat generalizations like this with skepticism, but because it is a descriptive statement and

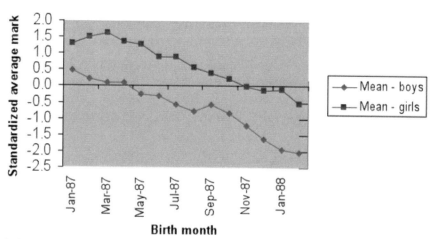

FIGURE 7.3.

not predictive or associated with value, prejudice, or inevitability, we accept it as a statement of fact: girls mature earlier at this stage in our culture. Given this, the fact that girls outperformed boys on the standardized test confirms the validity of the test.

The chart also makes it quite evident that the relative-age effect in birth-month achievement is apparent for both genders. There is one small departure from the aggregated chart pattern presented earlier. In this gender pattern, the girls' trend line, March was the month with the highest aggregate score. The boys' trend line did not spike upward to March and then decline thereafter.

The best explanation for this deviation is the one that created the trend lines in the first place. Parents are more likely to hold back immature children, and boys are more likely to be immature. Consequently, the girls' trend line shows the inclusion of a higher percentage of second January and February children, and hence the suppressed scores in their trend line in January and February. Further, boys are retained more frequently than are girls, and the system tests are grade tests rather than age tests. Therefore many of the very young boys had already been retained prior to being in grade three when the test was written, and their influence on the trend line was substantially minimized.

A different result emerged in the study of achievement in mathematics where boys scored higher than girls. Efforts are widespread to address this historic trend, and compensatory programs for girls are increasingly common. For example, some schools have launched all-girl classes and some school districts provide all-girl schools.

Universities, too, are making a concerted effort to increase female participation in degree programs specializing in mathematics and science because so many professions require participation and high levels of success in these disciplines. This is laudable and should be encouraged, but it is alarming that the same concern and subsequent effort are not evident in language arts, where girls repeatedly and significantly outperform boys.

Figure 7.4 below, which depicts scores in mathematics, demonstrates that both genders had a decline in achievement associated with birth month. Second, with the exception of March, boys' achievement was higher than females. Finally, the disparity in the first January and February for each gender verifies the conclusion stated for language arts. Many of the younger boys

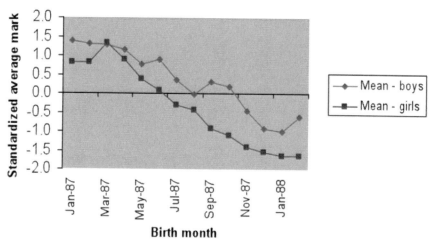

FIGURE 7.4.

were already held out of school for one year, and therefore the male population in that group comprises those boys who matured more quickly.

CHANGE NEEDS A CRISIS

The focus thus far has been on the effect that birth month has on the achievement levels of young students. The data reveals that it is unfair for a student to be born later in the registration time period and then be grouped on the basis of an annual, single-date entry point for each school year. To create a fairer situation, one or more of three things needs to happen: parents will have to practice more strategic family planning, rule makers will have to rethink the basis on which school-entry rules are established, or educators will have to rethink their practices for engaging children in the education system.

This assumes that society doesn't shrug an apathetic and disengaged shoulder, saying, "That's life, nobody said that it is going to be fair!" Such reasoning would go on to say, "After all, we have operated with this situation for generations and many educators were aware of the effect but never made a huge public issue about it, so why now?"

Why now? Because our forefathers made decisions in the past with the knowledge that was available to them. No large-scale, reliable database existed to inform decisions. Why now? Because the public today demands action in the face of evidence and transparency when accountability issues are at stake. Until recently, the educator's public creed was "students first" and "we are in this for the kids." If this remains true, and has meaning, then the rules related to enrollment will have to change.

Jean Monnet's (Mauldin, 2011) famous quote reminds us, however, that logic in the public arena is not any more inevitable than it is in our private lives: "People only accept change in necessity and see necessity only in crisis." This book is intended to help define and publicize the crisis in the hope that students truly are first in our thinking. The story does not end here.

The key points made in this chapter are:

- Older students' achievement is higher than that of younger ones on standardized tests.
- Properly constructed standardized tests provide accurate data on student achievement depicting significant differences by birth month.
- It is an unconscionable abuse of authority for leaders to admit groups of students into a class when it is known their chances of success are significantly reduced.
- Teachers perceived a significant difference between students born earlier than later in the school year, even though the issue of age difference was not before them when they did their evaluation.
- Relative-age effect in birth-month achievement is apparent for both genders.

8

Getting Older Doesn't Make It Go Away

KNOWING ABOUT UNFAIRNESS REQUIRES ACTION

Once the crisis of unfairness is known, a crisis of conscience emerges. Frequently parents are unaware of the decision-making processes in the education system and the way in which the system imposes screens to identify students it wishes to channel into a particular stream. Once a child begins a journey on a set pathway, there is little likelihood that he or she will be rerouted to a different pathway. Each fork in the road leaves the child with a reduced expectation, fewer career options, and ultimately a less fulfilling and rewarding life than would have been the case in a truly open and fair system.

Anecdotal evidence of the relative-age effect has existed within the education system for a long time; yet few have undertaken research to define the problem and find solutions that will create a fair situation for all children, including specifically those who had the misfortune to be born at a time the system had unwittingly determined to be second class. Even the research that was done focused on birth-month data that was not correlated with achievement, which resulted from our practice of streaming children into twelve-month cohorts via an annual, single-date entry for registration.

Evidence is accumulating now which demonstrates that the longevity of the negative impact of relative-age effect goes beyond the early primary school grades and, indeed, follows the student for many years. The testing program in this research is for grades three, six, and nine and, therefore, it is possible to track student achievement over time. Educators, in particular, will want to know the extent to which the grade three student achievement results are replicated in later years.

By the time students reach grade six the slope of the trend line decreases slightly, as figure 8.1 shows. It also shows that the differences between the months are becoming blurred. Also the six years of data are less precise between the birth months than was evident in the grade three results, when there was little difference in test results for each month during the five years of data.

When grade nine results are reviewed as demonstrated in figure 8.1, the pattern of conformity in a given month is even less obvious. Not only does the trend line have less of a slope but there is considerably more variation in student month-by-month scores during the five years. With the birth-month effect less evident in grade nine test scores, some people might interpret this as sufficient proof that, over time, the negative effects of relative age achievement are minimized.

Such an interpretation would raise the question as to whether or not it is necessary for the education system to undergo significant change when the disadvantage disappears over time and impacts a smaller proportion of the population. By extrapolation, one could say that by the time a person is thirty or forty, surely there is no difference between those born in January and those born in September or December. Therefore, is it really necessary to undertake

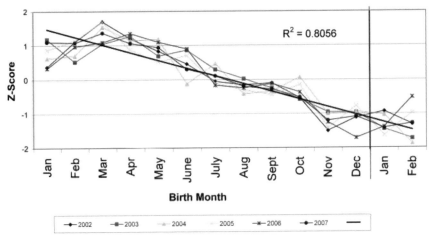

FIGURE 8.1.

any change for what may appear as a phenomenon disadvantaging only a very small minority of the population?

The data in figure 8.2 would appear to provide even more evidence for the skeptics. However, several factors are not readily discernible, which require a nuanced interpretation of the data. It is true that maturity, which can be attributed to birth month, should become less a factor over time as the breadth and depth of life experiences become more and more influential. But stating this rather obvious point is quite different than stating there is not a negative legacy effect to our current enrollment policy.

There is across the educational system a significant emphasis on getting the lower-achieving students up to grade level, which we have labeled already as the *moral imperative* of the school system. Anecdotal evidence suggests that we expend considerably more support and effort at the lower end for bringing achievement up to grade level than is expended at the upper end of the learning continuum.

There is a tendency to orient classroom instruction at the average student in the class and, with so many students functioning below grade level as they progress through the school system, the average quickly slips below what should be the appropriate level of instruction for the identified grade.

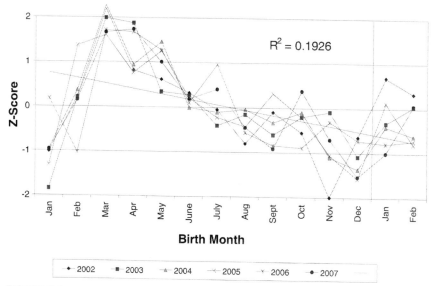

FIGURE 8.2.

In other words, educators constantly face pressure to water down grade level standards in order to accommodate the disproportionate number of weak students as cohorts move through the grades.

The subtle pressure the moral imperative imposes on teachers to water down the curriculum is evident from conversations involving educators in the different grade levels in schools. There is less likelihood that educators will make critical comments about the level of preparation provided to students within their own school. This tendency to avoid criticizing peers evident in educators changes, however, when students change buildings during their progress through the school system.

In meetings with educators in schools beginning with grade four, a significant message was that students graduating from the primary school (K–3) serving their area do not generally possess the skills necessary for success in grade four. A similar message, but even more strongly stated, came from middle school educators inheriting the elementary school graduates. Senior high school educators went to even greater lengths to state strongly how unprepared their students were when they arrived via the feeder system.

In summary, teachers and administrators who work with higher grades in a different school routinely express overwhelming dissatisfaction with the level of preparedness students have when they come to learn. Teachers in buildings with the lower-grade-level students felt defensive about this criticism and articulated many reasons why their students were falling behind in their abilities to perform up to grade expectation.

Therefore it is not surprising that figure 8.1 above depicting student achievement by birth month in grade six has more bounce within the results than is evident in grade three. These system tests are grade tests, and there are many students writing the grade six tests who really are not at the grade six level in their learning. Rather they qualify to be called a "grade six student" because of their age. The curriculum has been "dumbed down" to accommodate the growing list of students moving through the graded structure, while not having the skills necessary for demonstrating the curricular outcomes for their grade placement.

An earlier chapter described how grade inflation obscured the effect of relative-age effect and reduced the likelihood of parents becoming too alarmed. Social promotion is a similarly pernicious evil which has greatly reduced accountability and obscured the levels of failure that exist in our educational system.

Social Promotion Hides the Effect

Social promotion or, as some call it, "continuous pass," is now a significant issue in education. Its acceptance and use became increasingly widespread in the latter half of the twentieth century and to the point where it is simply unacceptable. There is a fine line involved in making a decision to retain a child or placing pressure on the school system to incorporate significant improvement efforts to ensure that the student achieves up to grade level.

Indeed, the No Child Left Behind legislation introduced in 2002 in the United States sought to undercut this practice because, as this policy gained favor with educators, classrooms of students experienced a widening range in levels of student achievement. For example, a grade five class of students likely included students functioning at several grade levels both above and below in addition to students achieving at the grade five level.

By grade seven the range in achievement levels is larger, and in grade nine larger still. A rule of thumb for a typical classroom is a spread in student achievement roughly equivalent to the grade nomenclature—e.g., grade five would have roughly a five-grade spread in student achievement, grade nine would have a nine-grade spread, and so on. In numerous discussions with the general public they find this situation to be incredible and even ridiculous.

Of course, the spread in student achievement could be more complex because in some instances there will also be a student with exceptional needs and therefore an outlier. Anecdotal evidence from one school administrator indicated how a grade one boy in his school was reading successfully commensurate with a grade six student. This posed quite a challenge during class discussions because the rest of the class was prone to defer to him because they recognized his reading level made him considerably more knowledgeable about issues being discussed.

At the same time, a class of grade six students in the same school had one student functioning at the grade two reading level and another one reading at a senior-high level. This latter student could be seen going home on Friday after school from the school library with heavy reading material under his arm, with books such as *The Rise and Fall of the Third Reich*. He acknowledged how this grade six class truly was an outlier experience because the significant challenge in teaching these students could be managed only through individualized instruction activities.

These scenarios came from a relatively small elementary school with only four classrooms for six grades. The class was also a split grade of all grade five and six students in the school. In the end, this challenging teaching assignment made the teacher better because it required him to develop and utilize techniques in individualized instruction. All students experienced educational programming designed for their level of instruction.

The point here is that there is a substantial range in learning within any class of students. In this study, approximately one in five grade three students was unable to demonstrate grade level expectations on system achievement tests. In 2010, Ontario's (Canada's largest province) grade six results indicated that approximately three in ten students were unable to demonstrate competency in reading, and four out of ten students in mathematics. By the end of grade nine in this study, almost one in three in math and one in five for language arts were not able to meet grade level standards. They were, however, progressing with their age peers.

With this information in hand, it becomes clear that the variation in the data evident in figure 8.2 is attributable to a number of factors. Too many extraneous factors have now come into play. There remains a disadvantage based on month of birth, but the practice of social promotion widens the achievement range within the cohort of students being tested. The data is further confounded because not all children are promoted, of course. In this study, schools retained one in six students by the ninth grade. This further corrupts the potential for this data to maintain a consistent, gradual trend line.

The impact of birth month is increasingly lost in this cacophony. Many students have fallen off of the proverbial school bus as it rolls through the school system, and incorporating their test results is the confounding factor demonstrating an increased variability in the chart depicting birth-month achievement. With such a substantial percentage of students struggling to keep up with their age cohort, it is not unusual for teachers to focus on the lower end of the achievement scale. This is their moral imperative!

Indeed, this study found evidence demonstrating that only 1 percent of students were officially accelerated whereas 17 percent were decelerated. It is vital to understand that this high percentage of decelerated students did not include the undetermined percentage of students moving through the system because of the widespread practice of social promotion. While there seems to be all sorts of compensatory effort for the weak students, there is a lack of emphasis on ensuring that talented students experience intellectual challenge commensurate with their abilities.

Some educators may object to a criticism of the current system based on the theory that even though there are problems with vertical acceleration, they are addressed by the presence of horizontal acceleration in the form of "enrichment." This is a vacuous argument given the fact that deceleration is seventeen times more likely than acceleration. Having visited more than 20,000 classrooms, it can be stated with reasonable confidence that most educators do not use individualized instruction, especially in the higher grades.

Therefore, when teachers are teaching their classes and there are so many students functioning academically below their assigned grade level, combined with the considerable attention by politicians on students who are achieving below grade level, it is quite logical to expect that instruction is centered more at the lower level of the graded curriculum. As a result, more talented students are being left behind where they could and should be because their advanced educational needs are not being addressed.

The implication on test results is that variances in student achievement are reduced because of the lack of high expectations for our most academically talented students. This point was recently reinforced in a system consultation ("Speak-Out") with high school students who identified lack of engagement with their schoolwork as their primary concern with the education system.

The "lack of challenge" issue is part of the reason why the slope of the grade nine trend line is not as steep as in earlier grades. Teaching to the average in the class produces an insidious negative influence on the education system's commitment to high expectations. Yes, there are some higher expectations, but only for a select group. This phenomenon will be discussed in more detail later.

There remains yet another issue that has an even greater impact on reducing the slope of the line between the birth months. Simply stated, large numbers of students have disappeared from the cohort of students. Each year, many students "fall off the bus" and, because the system tests are grade tests, they do not register an impact on these tests with their age cohort. In other words, a grade three student struggling in school may subsequently be retained and, therefore, write the grade six and nine system tests as an older member of another cohort of students.

Having been held back in school at least one year provides these students with some added intellectual development necessary for success on the tests. If the system tests were an age test, the slope of the line would be even more evident because many of the retained students born in the latter half of the registration period would have written the test with lower levels of achievement.

The degree to which grade retention occurs, then, is important information in the story of the long-term impact of relative-age effect. In order to assess this, we undertook a longitudinal study of students entering kindergarten in the 1995–1996 school year. These students were followed until they reached high school to determine retention rates. At the conclusion of the initial school year, very few students retained in kindergarten were born in January through May (see figure 8.3).

Student Retention Magnifies the Problem

Viewing the birth-month data beyond the month of May, we see a gradual increase in retention rates through the month of August before there is a steep incline that carries on to December and then an even steeper incline to February of the following year. Therefore, while the overall retention in kin-

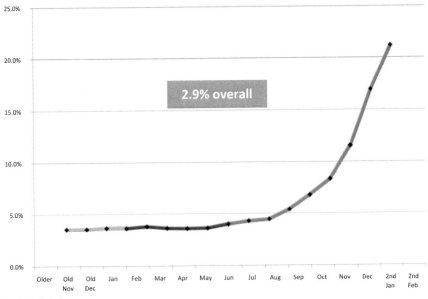

FIGURE 8.3.

dergarten for the cohort was 2.9 percent, the rate for December birth-month students was 15 percent and the second-February students at 20 percent. Clearly teachers found that children born in the latter portion of the registration year face a serious disadvantage and a greater need to be retained.

Figure 8.3 demonstrates a distressing illustration about an unfair situation in our nation's most valuable resource. At a time when social promotion was gaining prominence and retention was becoming an unpopular remedy for low achievement, school staff still retained a substantial percentage of students. The tragedy is that the vast majority of these retentions, and all the concomitant social ramifications, occurred with students born in the second half of the registration period. The story becomes more disturbing a year later.

When the same cohort of students completed grade one, schools retained an additional 2 percent of students across all birth months (see figure 8.4). Again the retention rate was fairly flat from January through June before it increased sharply during the birth months in the latter half of the year. For the December birth month, another 10 percent of students were retained, and the second-February birth-month students had another 17 percent retention rate. Examining the left side of figure 8.4, it is evident that some of the grade one students were already older than the grade one cohort group

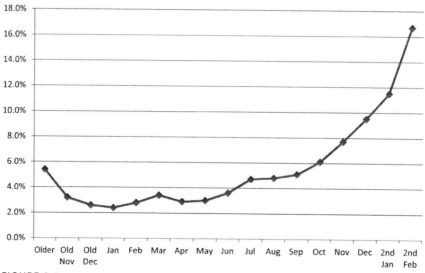

FIGURE 8.4.

under investigation. Therefore, they were in their third year of school, counting kindergarten, and the system had already retained them twice.

Retention rates for the cohort increased in grade two, as depicted in figure 8.5 below, decreased somewhat from the earlier two years. In schools that were still routinely retaining students, their modus operandi appears to have been to retain sooner rather than later. Nevertheless, they retained another 2.2 percent of the original student cohort with all months at more than 1 percent; and the December birth-month children experiencing another 4 percent retention rate.

Again, these retentions only occurred in schools where the practice of retaining students was still employed. There were also many schools where the social promotion philosophy prevailed, and these students are not contained within the data even though they, too, would have been functioning below grade level. By the end of grade nine more than 30 percent of the students were unable to pass the system mathematics test. From this we are able to deduce that social promotion was every bit as prevalent as retention.

By the time the 1995–1996 kindergarten cohort of students left grade nine, the retention rate reached 13.8 percent of students participating in the formal learning program of grades one through nine (see figure 8.6). If the

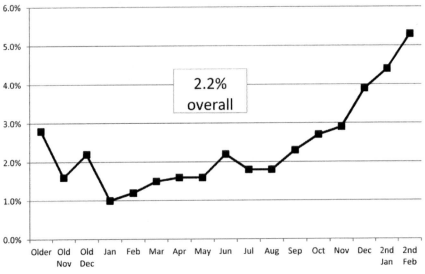

FIGURE 8.5.

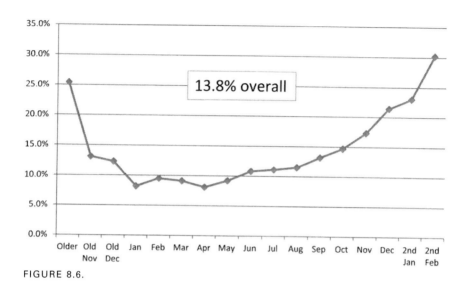

13.8% overall

FIGURE 8.6.

kindergarten students are added to the formal grades, the retention rate for all students entering the school system for kindergarten through grade nine was 16.7 percent or one in six students. December birth-month retentions were almost three times the January ones.

In some respects this data is staggering, because many schools have a philosophical perspective which is opposed to student retention, and those students whom they socially promote are not included in the retentions. It bears repeating that this data represents only actual retentions because data on students proceeding as a result of social promotion was not collected.

Considerable controversy exists within the education community about retention and, hence, there is not a regional policy. Indeed, many school districts find this to be a contentious issue and delegate policies in this area to individual schools, so there is variation in practice even within school districts. Nevertheless, review of the data demonstrates clearly that students with birth months in the first half of the year are less likely to be retained than those in the second half.

Explaining the data using actual numbers makes even more clear the size of the problem by giving students a number, if not a name. In the region under investigation, there were approximately 44,000 students in the cohort. Ten years later, 17 percent, or approximately 7,500 students, had been retained at least once. Instead of taking ten years to progress through the K–9 system, these students took eleven or more years.

These retained students required considerable resources from the system. Based on an average class size of twenty students, an additional 375 classes were needed to accommodate the retained students. The school system had to hire additional teachers for these classes, appoint more administrative support staff, allocate more classroom space, and provide more custodial services.

Based on this region's expenditure of approximately $6B per year on the K–12 education system, the current cost of having one in six students spending an additional year in school is approximately $140M per grade cohort. This is a conservative "guesstimate" because most retention occurs in the early years when class sizes are considerably less than twenty students per class. The situation in the other Canadian provinces would be quite similar, which means that resources required to deal with the student failure nationally amounts to well over a billion dollars.

Much of this added expense occurs unnecessarily and can be traced back to the negative impact of relative-age effect. Hence, not only is there a significant personal loss of self-esteem and a significant social loss of missed opportunity and contribution, there is also a substantial financial cost to the country. One is tempted to say that we could avoid all of this if the government and educators could convince parents to plan more carefully to have spring-born babies. Alternatively, and realistically, these problems can and should be avoided by changing some simple, basic, but unfair rules.

Even small steps could make a difference. Change could occur immediately with little pushback from educators or the public if school systems with a fourteen-month registration window reduced it to twelve months. The story described in the figures above demonstrates that the inclusion of these very young students dramatically increases the risk of failure. Schools were forced to retain 30 percent of second-February birth-month students in schools permitting second-February enrollment. It is important to keep in mind that this data only tracked students the schools actually retained; it did not include those they socially promoted, which could only have added to the percentage of struggling students.

There are few rules in the education system which have a greater deleterious impact on students than single-date entry, twelve-month cohorts. How long will the unfair treatment of such a large percentage of the student population be tolerated before the public challenges the system to change? Once it happens it may not be pleasant. Until now, educators have generally avoided malpractice suits, but the issue of bringing young students into an environment that predisposes them to failure, or at least to an unacceptably high risk of failing, has the aura of malpractice about it.

Birth Month Reaches into Adulthood

It is not just the younger, underperforming students who are at risk, however. Test results discussed earlier reveal that achievement is also reduced for students who are not retained. As logical as this fact may now be, this impact is also overlooked. Greater percentages of these later-birth-month students will not qualify for higher-stream or advanced courses in senior high school programs which, in turn, reduces their potential to qualify for university programs. The consequence of being a student born in the latter part of the year can result in a lifelong impact.

The impact of birth month on a student entering senior high school is clear from data gathered in the United Kingdom. A declining trend line depicts falling achievement by month of birth for students aged fourteen to sixteen years (typically grades ten and eleven), who are in the General Certificate of Secondary Education (GCSE) program. Students enrolled in the GCSE have taken compulsory school-leaving exams since the 1980s, so the body of data is well established.

Generally, students take between six and eight GCSE courses annually and have some degree of latitude in what they study. However, English and mathematics are required for moving forward into higher education. Grades of C to A allow students to move into the A-level program, whereas marks from D to G channel students toward apprenticeship, other training, or work. These examinations are high stakes, meaning that the final student mark is based exclusively on the examination and is not adjusted by an assessment from a teacher.

The data from these GCSEs demonstrate the longer-term effect of birth-month achievement as students near graduation in the United Kingdom. The data demonstrates that student grade point averages are highest for students born in September and trend downward for each successive month. In the United Kingdom the twelve-month cohort is September to August of the following calendar year.

Birth month even impacts the oldest students in the secondary program. Students in the United Kingdom write A-level examinations in three subjects which are more specialized; good scores are required for entrance into university. As is the case with the GCSE, the A-level examination is marked centrally without any input from the classroom teacher. Approximately one-third of the school-age population participates in the examinations.

The results tell the same story as the GCSE examination. In this case, the trend line follows the same downward slope, but the correlation is with the numbers who write the exam. While it is open to all, decreasing numbers qualify to sit the exams based on age: the farther away the child is from a September birth, the less likely he or she is to write the exam. This means that 35 percent of September-born babies write the exam, as opposed to 30 percent of those born twelve months later in August.

These findings in the United Kingdom indicate the residual negative effect of birth month right to the end of a student's K–12 education. Michael Barber (2008), who led the accountability office for the national government, examined the long-term effect that schooling had on children. His conclusion was that literacy in primary school was a key factor of performance in all subjects at age sixteen. Therefore, the degree of success in the early years when birth month is a factor remains a factor throughout a child's primary and secondary education.

The next obvious question has to do with the impact of birth month on students at the postsecondary level. Gladwell (2008) reported that in the United States, participation in the highest stream of four-year colleges demonstrated that students belonging to the relatively youngest group in their class are underrepresented in the more prestigious colleges by almost 12 percent. Therefore, the initial disadvantage resulting from birth month does not go away with time; furthermore, for many students, the disadvantage becomes the difference between attending a prestigious institution, with its exceptional placement record, and a less prestigious institution, with its record of less prestigious employment following graduation.

In the United Kingdom, the data also demonstrated approximately a 4 percent variance in higher-education participation rates between the September and August birth months. The aggregated data indicates a plateau during the middle months ranging from December to May, but months at both ends of the trend line depict a consistently declining level of participation that demonstrates a disadvantage for students born closer to the end of the registration year.

The results in a Canadian study are similar. The University of Alberta, one of Canada's most prestigious universities, provided data demonstrating its birth-month registrants. The data reflects age at first registration in the university with students typically entering in September. The university examined actual monthly birth rates for its region and compared registrations by birth month.

The advantage for students born early in the registration period is clearly evident. Average registrations for the first quarter (January through March) of the year were approximately 10 percent higher than expected based on actual births. Average registrations for students born in the last quarter (October through December) were approximately 17 percent below expectation based on actual births. The variance of approximately 27 percent between the first and fourth quarters, again, demonstrates a significant disadvantage for students born near the end of the registration year.

Efforts to reform education have paid relatively little attention toward the issue of relative-age effect. One of the intentions of this book is to demonstrate the lasting impact of the effect in years beyond primary school education. There is very little information relative to the correlation between birth month and achievement in adulthood, which is not surprising given the lack of concern about the unfairness evident to children born late in the registration period.

However, there is some preliminary data, and it confirms the negative legacy of our current practice. Michael Barber provided some information on adulthood from an analysis he conducted in the United Kingdom. His research determined that literacy at age seven was strongly correlated with earnings at age thirty-seven. In other words, the impact of literacy levels for students leaving grade one, where student success relative to birth month is very well documented, remains well into adulthood. Assuming that earnings are a valid measure for participation in more demanding careers, relative-age effect remains a constraining factor in many lives.

To this point in the chapter, the analysis regarding relative-age effect has been focused on the academic success of students. Some research has also suggested there are social implications for the students, especially in regard to self-esteem. In a study of more than ten thousand children aged five to fifteen in the United Kingdom, Robert Goodman (2003) found that "The younger children in a school are at a slightly greater psychiatric risk than older children. Increased awareness by teachers of the relative age of their pupils and a more flexible approach to children's progression through school might reduce the number of children with impairing psychiatric disorders in the general population."

Thompson et al. published an article in the *Canadian Journal of Psychiatry* (1999) in which they reported on previous research related to relative-age effect and youth suicide. The authors concluded that:

> Relative age is strongly related to school performance and success in sports. The present study demonstrates that the relative-age-effect is also a factor in youth suicide. It is suggested that the higher incidence of youth suicide in the group of relatively younger school children may have resulted from poorer school performance, which in turn led to lowered confidence and self-esteem.

It is deeply sobering and troubling to realize that, because of school convention, simply being born in the wrong month raises the chance of lower confidence, poorer self-esteem, and suicide.

Many people are aware that the education system disadvantages younger children, but perhaps the degree of unfairness or its effects are unknown. Schools have operated under these rules for so long that everyone is socialized to see the convention as normal, reasonable, and unavoidable. If there is evidence that demonstrates a negative impact on our nation's brightest and best, might that be sufficient to spark reform?

The key points made in this chapter are:

- The negative impact of relative-age effect goes beyond the early primary school grades and, indeed, follows the student for many years.
- There is, across the educational system, a significant emphasis on getting the lower-achieving students up to grade level, which we have labeled as the *moral imperative* of the school system.
- Educators constantly face pressure to water down grade level standards in order to accommodate the disproportionate number of weak students as cohorts move through the grades.
- Teachers and administrators who work with higher grades in a different school routinely express overwhelming dissatisfaction with the level of preparedness students have when they come to learn.

- Social promotion is a pernicious evil which has greatly reduced accountability and obscured the levels of failure that exist in our educational system.
- There is a substantial range in learning within any class of students.
- While there seems to be all sorts of compensatory effort for the weak students, there is a lack of emphasis on ensuring that talented students experience intellectual challenge commensurate with their abilities.
- Students with birth months in the first half of the year are less likely to be retained than those in the second half.
- Findings in the United Kingdom indicate the residual negative effect of birth month right to the end of a student's K–12 education.

9

Education's Glass Ceiling

OUR BRIGHTEST AND BEST ARE HAMPERED

The metaphor of a "glass ceiling" arose in everyday conversation to describe in picturesque terms the barrier talented women and minorities faced if they wished to advance in their careers. Over time the definition has broadened to include virtually anyone facing artificial barriers that interfere with advancement. In the field of education, the metaphorical "glass ceiling" is the unseen yet unbreachable barrier that keeps high-achieving students from realizing their academic potential, and it is another one of the serious negative effects of our current practice of single-date entry, twelve-month cohorts. This book has already demonstrated a partial, unbreachable barrier in the deceleration-acceleration continuum.

In an analysis of the longitudinal study done over the period 1996 to 2007, we found that the school system decelerated one in six students who had entered the system in 1996 by the time they had reached grade nine. Meanwhile, the system accelerated only one in one hundred students during the same period of time. For simplicity purposes, we can say that decelerating students on the basis of their achievement is six times more frequent than acceleration.

The prevailing idea in education has been that students should remain with age peers; yet so obsessed are we with struggling students and the desire to be kind, fair, and generous with them, that almost 17 percent were retained in spite of stated adherence to the idea that students remain with age peers. It is almost certain that schools would have retained a significantly higher percent on the inability to keep up, but the prevailing idea of promotion led them to advance many more than they should have. This interpretation is justified not only by anecdotal evidence, which is convincing in itself, but also by statistical data. For example, by the end of grade nine almost one in three students was unable to pass the math assessment.

Data reported in this book almost always reports on the average, which is necessary for the education systems' rule makers. By definition, some students will be above and some below "average," and there are always exceptions. Schools are quick to laud publicly the educational achievement of a few high performers. These public pronouncements then provide a false sense of security that the education system is high performing.

The averages tell a more accurate and more depressing story, and parents need to consider these messages when making decisions about their school and their child. Outliers exist in every distribution. In hockey, relative-age effect demonstrated the majority of NHL hockey players were born in the first quarter of the year, but Mario Lemieux and Sidney Crosby, two superstars, were born in the latter half of the registration year. In education, dealing with averages will always result in exceptions, or outliers. Parents require information on both averages and the outliers so that a child has opportunity to maximize their potential.

It is known that differences in physical development are significant for those aspiring to excel in athletics. Earlier it was noted that there are parallels between intellectual and physical development when looked at from a twelve-month-cohort perspective. Many rules in registration are built around the January-to-December calendar. The earliest month for registration into sports as well as school is usually January, resulting in the average child born in this month becoming the oldest, biggest, and smartest in the age cohort. The first step in good family planning is self-evident, albeit impractical and unlikely to be taken seriously.

What can and should be taken seriously? How can parents cope with the relative-age effect? In addition to the conscious messages of affirmation, the child is exposed to many subliminal messages of mixed quality. Developing an appropriate mindset is the next key consideration. Too frequently a parent's mindset is focused on getting their child into the school system as quickly as possible. Once the child is in school, parents enjoy certain freedoms including the significant one that comes from knowing that their child is in a safe and nurturing environment for some six hours a day. However, it is not as safe and nurturing as parents assume. In addition to the conscious messages of affirmation, the child is exposed to many subliminal messages of mixed quality.

Children are not oblivious to the success experienced by others in their class. They can soon discern for themselves who the "smart" kids in the class are and where they fit relative to the various abilities of these classmates. Their assessment of their relative status informs their subliminal mind, which in turn shapes their self-concept. In this process it is only logical that there is a strong likelihood of younger students acquiring perceptions that they are not as successful as the majority of peers. Merely hoping that this information might inspire them to do better at this stage may not be realistic when the issue is associated with developmental lag.

Consequently, as a result of this mental and psychological process going on in the heart and mind of their child, it is important that parents have a clear and realistic idea about what is happening in the early years of school. With a child born in the months near the end of the annual cycle—i.e., October to December—an appropriate mindset is to think about delaying the child's entry into the school system for a year. On too many occasions parents merely adopt an intuitive position that a practice utilized for centuries must be in their child's best interests. Research proves otherwise!

Opting to delay is not the norm, so it is a wise parent and courageous parent who flows against the stream of public opinion, even though the data is clear that the considerable majority of students the school system retains are born in the latter portion of the year. But this is also a tip-off that children not identified for retention may still be significantly behind older peers. Social promotion does not have to be the alternate strategy. As the decision date for entering the school system draws near, parents are faced with many conflicting emotions and opinions from relatives and friends.

Parents who are in a decision-making situation will benefit from turning to early childhood educators for advice and counsel. In doing so, they need to keep in mind there is a system-wide inclination to avoid disappointing either the child or the parent with a message which suggests delay. After all, it is readily apparent that many children born in this time frame are successful when they enter school even as the younger students in the class. Herein lies the difficulty: they may be successful, but are they as successful as they could be? How much of their potential was not achieved simply because they entered too early?

One possible solution to working through the myriad of issues is to ascertain the degree to which the child is able to succeed with tasks undertaken by children born near the beginning of the school year. It does not help to observe comparators born in the latter half of the year, because many will be successful in school but will not enjoy the degree of success generated by those beginning the formal learning process when they were more mature. Many children travel through their school programs always experiencing the threshold of success but not the high degree of success necessary for getting into more invigorating career-oriented programs.

Our Focus on the Weak Weakens the Strong

Maximizing educational potential is more than merely crossing the annual threshold of success. Parents reading this and knowing that their child was born in the first half of the year may have the attitude that this issue has no implications for their child. Unfortunately this is not the case, and parents will benefit from knowing the implications of how one situation might impact another. There are unintended consequences to our schools' current pursuit of the moral imperative.

Data presented earlier demonstrates that teachers with larger percentages of weak students tend to give students higher marks than are actually warranted: this is a condition known as grade inflation. This practice may be viewed as motivating students to higher levels of achievement when, in fact, the opposite is true. There is considerable research demonstrating that the greater the grade inflation the lower are the marks that students receive on standardized tests.

An alarming example occurred during one term as superintendent where the highest-performing school on the provincial tests recorded 37 percent of students in the class as receiving a letter grade of A or B on their report card. The school with the lowest results on the provincial tests had 75 percent of students receiving A or B on their report cards. Clearly, curriculum standards were not assessed consistently in the school with such large numbers of students receiving A or B.

Grade inflation acts as a demotivator for students, who tend to develop an unrealistic and inflated opinion of their ability. The result is that they spend less time studying and less effort working. It also acts as a demotivator to well-intentioned parents who believe that their child is performing exceptionally well in school. As a consequence, they spend less time helping them with homework and less effort in acquiring special tutoring.

The significant range in student ability can also cause teachers to aim their classroom instruction to the lower end of the achievement scale, which has already been referred to as the moral imperative of the school system. When there is a proliferation of weaker students in the class, instruction tends to be geared more to these weaker students. There exists a logical empathetic reaction toward focusing more on students who are struggling than those who are experiencing success even though the success is less than justified by the student's ability.

The evidence of this tendency is demonstrated in reviewing system tests and examining the percentage of students who had achieved a standard in one grade but, three years later, were no longer able to achieve or maintain that standard. In this study, 7 percent of the grade six student population achieving the Acceptable Standard, which is equivalent to achieving a "pass" mark, in literacy and numeracy three years earlier in grade three were no longer able to demonstrate the standard.

However, at the Standard of Excellence, which is equivalent to achieving outcomes in the A range, 45 percent of students dropped below the standard they had achieved in grade three.

When we did an analysis of the students who were progressing from grade six to grade nine, similar results emerged. In this comparison, the percentage of students dropping out of the Standard of Excellence was four and a half times greater than those dropping out of the Acceptable Standard. Whereas only 10 percent of students could no longer achieve at the Acceptable Standard, 45 percent lost their Standard of Excellence designation.

The schools' commitment toward achieving the moral imperative at the expense of maintaining their commitment to achieving the high standards of the curriculum was the norm across virtually all sixty-two school districts in the region. In other words, the significant numbers of students who were struggling to keep pace with curriculum expectations were constantly pulling down the level of classroom instruction so that expectations for the grade were not met.

In order to determine how widespread the problem was between grade six and nine, we examined the results of each school district. Only students in the school district taking both the grades six and nine standardized tests in mathematics were included so that a school district's performance could be measured on the basis of the students being there for the entire period of time. In other words, the specific school district was entirely responsible for the student's instruction during the three-year period.

Only one school district improved, and that was by less than 1 percent. This means that slightly more students attained the Acceptable Standard than dropped below it during the period of investigation. All other districts had more students fall below the Acceptable Standard than move above it. Across the region the midpoint was a net loss of 16 percent, although the districts ranged from a net loss of 25 percent to the one district that had a slightly positive score. In spite of effort and funding, the moral imperative did not happen!

A similarly negative picture emerged when we examined the results for students over a six-year period. All sixty-two districts had more students retrogress than progress, with one district showing a net loss of more than 50 percent. Almost one-half of the districts saw more than 20 percent of their students slip below the Acceptable Standard they had achieved earlier in grade three. Incredibly this loss occurred during a time frame when the region was decreasing class sizes through the hiring of 13 percent more teachers. It could be argued that reducing class size ensured that the results were not worse, but the evidence, such as it is, argues the other way and makes it imperative that we look for other solutions.

Standardized Tests Tell a Valid Story

This kind of data explains why some stakeholder organizations in the education community oppose standardized testing: they tell a story that makes it difficult, if not impossible, to explain away the tired platitudes and blame shifting. Teachers develop the tests, and the region diligently field-tests every question for validity and reliability. Educational leaders in the districts are therefore unable to excuse themselves or their schools from the results which emerge. Quantitative data can be threatening because it has the capacity to demonstrate a far more encompassing picture than does qualitative data.

It is also important to remember that system-wide tests provide percentages of students who have not demonstrated sufficient understanding of grade level standards. This is a consistent measurement because all students across the region are held to the same standard. Teachers' assessments are neither as consistent nor as grounded in the objectives of the curriculum, as has already been demonstrated. Individual teachers apply their own interpretation of the standards, and there is no check on their biases. This is known by district leaders and teachers, but the social pressures to preserve the status quo are so great that the decision makers essentially "plug their ears" and "close their eyes."

This systemic rejection of logic and wisdom led one teacher, who was faced with the assignment of assessing and reporting on student achievement, to say, "In our (school district) students have to be two or three grade levels below grade placement before we can report them as being below grade level." This is an excellent example of how social promotion promotes grade inflation.

Parents are told that their child is working at grade level even though the teacher's assessment is that their child is two or three grade levels behind. Of course the parent is left with the mistaken impression that their child is coping and, on that basis, likely not creating an instructional disturbance in the school. If the parents understood reality, there is a reasonable likelihood that they would pursue private tutoring to get their child back to grade level.

It is important to emphasize that system tests are based on the curriculum and developed with extensive involvement of classroom teachers from around the region. Each item is constructed with the assistance of teacher panels and is thoroughly field-tested to make sure that the item is valid and reliable. Once the test is written, each item is reviewed to make sure that it has met standards which are higher than standards used in international tests.

Many educators representing educational systems around the world visited our region's testing department to learn how to construct tests of similar quality. Further, test publishers have confided their perspectives that these tests are above the quality of tests from their own companies and used in the United States. Indeed, so highly regarded are these tests that the United States sent out an investigative team in 1993 and concluded their report to Congress with the words,

> Widespread teacher involvement . . . helps increase teachers' knowledge of curricula and instruction and aids in the development of tests that are compatible with good classroom instruction. In contrast, U.S. teachers do not typically play key roles in the development of commercial or state tests and, thus, do not have access to similar experiences that hold the promise of improving both teaching and testing.

The quality of their work was reaffirmed in 2009 when officials working for the Secretary of Education requested that our region send a representative to meet with aides from the White House, Congress, and governors in order to explain how they could improve.

If the parents of children who are falling behind should be concerned, so should other parents whose children are not performing up to their potential. The data from these high-quality system tests demonstrates that a significantly higher percentage of students are falling below the Standard of Excellence than are falling below the Acceptable Standard. Success at the upper end is sacrificed to achieve "success," such as it is, with students working at the lower end. The moral compass is at work, which inherently causes the system to focus on the struggling students more than the ones who are very capable.

Implications of this analysis should send a signal to parents with children who are strong academically or, as some like to put it, gifted and talented. Simply assuming the school system will provide an education program that incorporates challenging schoolwork for capable students may be an unwise assumption. Parents may need to pursue other programs which have the ability to enrich their child, or risk negative consequences associated with their child's boredom and lack of engagement.

Another study in the region provided additional evidence from classroom teachers that showed they placed a disproportionate emphasis on helping the weak students progress. Teachers for all of the region's students in grades one through nine assessed their students as being either "above" or "below" grade level. This was the teacher's assessment based on whatever information the teacher chose to use as well as whatever the weightings the teacher applied to the information.

In these assessments, many times more students were assessed as "below" grade level than "above." Indeed, the ratios were approximately 7:1 except for language arts, where the ratio of males functioning "below" grade level was assessed as 17:1. It is logical that a fairly normal distribution would occur, but it was entirely illogical for such a skewed result to have occurred if there was not a serious problem with student-personalized learning where individual students progressed at his or her own pace.

The regional study of teacher assessment practices concluded with a comment from the researchers that "The qualitative data indicate that there are mixed expectations with respect to children with special needs . . . and that students who were gifted were not sufficiently challenged." Our brightest and best are being reined in and held back by a "glass ceiling" that mitigates against them achieving their potential. Every nation needs these gifted students to explore their talent to the fullest.

High Fliers Are Being Grounded

In the relative-age-effect discussion there is very little understanding of this "glass ceiling" effect evident in the literature to date. However, in 2011, a study in the United States (Xiang) emerged with a rather catchy promotional statement on the cover front cover: "The first US study to examine the performance of America's highest-achieving children over time at the individual-student level." Contained within the report was an even more probing question which asked, "Do high flyers maintain their altitude?"

This timely report tracked the outcomes of American students who were high flyers initially, but who "fell off the bus" several years later. Specifically, somewhat like this study, students were tracked by achievement groups. The first group was comprised of high flyers in grade three who were then followed up with a subsequent assessment in grade eight. The researchers tracked the second group from grade six to grade ten.

This national report indicated the percentage of students who "lost altitude" from high flyer status in grade three to grade eight. In math, 43 percent of students descended while in reading it was 44 percent. In the grade six to grade ten study, 30 percent descended in math and 48 percent descended in reading. The report concluded that "descenders" dropped from the ninety-fourth percentile to the seventy-seventh percentile or from the top 10 percent of their grade to the top 30 percent. Chester Finn, whom Xiang quotes, stated that:

> If America is to remain internationally competitive with other advanced nations, we need to maximize the potential of our top students. Yet many analysts worry that various policies and programs tend to level student achievement by focusing on the lowest-achieving students and ignoring, or worse, driving resources away from our strongest students.

Finn's warning and challenge are really an indictment of the social promotion/grade inflation/moral imperative philosophies of our day which inform and inspire decision makers. And no aspect of these well-meaning but errant ideas is more deleterious than the twelve-month, single-date entry cohort concept that cohabitates with them in the unquestioning minds of an uninformed public.

Figure 9.1 below categorizes students born in March and the second February by their standardized test scores in grade three. In effect, the age difference in the two groups is approximately eleven months, but what makes them particularly interesting is that they represent the highest and lowest points of achievement on the scale. Achievement levels are aggregated for the initial 0 to 29 percent range because numbers are relatively small, but the other students fell into categories created by deciles. The two bar lines represent "gains" in student achievement according to the two birth months.

Students in grade three scoring in the 60 to 69 and 70 to 79 percent ranges in grade three demonstrate approximately a 0 percent gain in achievement in grade nine. In other words, these students gained what was expected during the next six years of school, and achieved in grade nine at the same level as they achieved in grade three. Essentially they acquired six years of learning in six years.

Students scoring less than 60 percent in grade three recorded a "gain" for the average student. For example, students scoring in the 30 to 39 percent range in grade three improved their average mark by approximately 17 percent. This may be a good news story because the schools' efforts at improving low levels of student achievement were successful. However, this happy conclusion needs to be nuanced: is the gain sufficient? Is it what one would anticipate? Nevertheless, there was a gain!

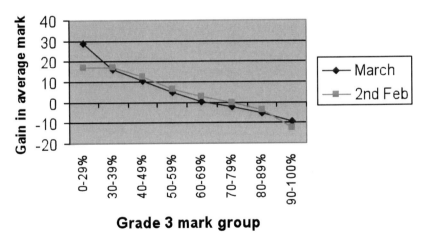

FIGURE 9.1.

Unfortunately there is also a "loss" or decline for a particular group of students. Those with a grade three mark in the nineties had their average grade nine mark decline by approximately 10 percent. Declining levels in student achievement were recorded for students in general who had achieved marks above 70. The schools' efforts toward improving achievement levels of low-performing students prevented high achievers from maintaining much less improving their success.

Figure 9.1 is also very significant because it demonstrates that students born in the second February did not gain on those born in the first February despite having so much opportunity to do so. Therefore, despite all of the schools' efforts to bring these very young students up to grade level they remained as far behind in grade nine as they were in grade three. Again, birth-month data demonstrates long-term disadvantage for the younger students.

There was one exception to the pattern of gains and declines diverging for the two age groups. Student test scores in grade three for the 0 to 29 percent range for both birth months demonstrated improved results in grade nine, but the older students (March) improved to a greater extent. In other words, the intensive assistance the schools provided to achieve the moral imperative of helping the lower-achieving students was particularly successful with the older, more mature students.

The chart also provides an insight into the bigger issue of an important enrollment date for children. The gain or decline between any two birth months that were exactly six years apart was virtually the same from grade three to grade nine in all scores that ranged from 30 to 100 percent. In other words, younger students were unable to overcome the deficit they had when they enrolled. Time did not ameliorate the negative impact, which began in the fall of the first year. Data from this chart alone should motivate school systems to caution parents about enrolling their young children at an early age.

Yes, there are exceptional children and extenuating circumstances, but the averages indicate that disadvantages are perpetuated for many years. This region during the period of this study required students to make major decisions about their high school courses at the end of grade nine, that is, before they entered high school. Once again this left younger students with their relatively lower achievement scores paying yet another price for their early start in school, as they were relegated to lower-stream courses in a school they had yet to attend. Ultimately these lower-stream courses limited students' access to universities.

Figure 9.1, then, portrays some good news regarding future success by grade nine for the weaker grade three students. However, many students were retained after grade three and wrote the grade nine test while taking seven years instead of six to reach grade nine. Therefore, some of the achievement gains occurring from grade three to grade nine for the lower-achieving students, when they were in grade three, can be attributed to the intellectual maturation gained in the additional year.

The central point is that efforts to achieve the imperative of improving achievement for the weaker students, who were mostly younger students, interfered with the achievement of stronger, mostly older students. This research and the recent study from the United States are the first studies to demonstrate an impact regarding relative-age effect on older and more capable students. Unfortunately, the effect is negative.

This chapter has demonstrated various long-term effects on the education system brought about by the combination of student achievement related to birth month and the annual, single-date entry system. Frequently, it has commented how the practice of social promotion has an impact on the data but that the impact has been unknown because there is no clearly defined policy in place for this region that permits scientific measurement. Nevertheless, it is now possible to say that social promotion masks the magnitude and seriousness of the relative-age effect.

During discussions with school administrators one explained the negativity of this masking effect by stating succinctly, "We need to help kids at the top more because our leaders in society are mostly from the top. Instead we go to the 'drowners' first because that is where we have the sense of urgency." My argument is certainly not that the future "leaders," as the administrator put it, receive "more help" than the "drowners," but rather that all children receive the help they need to achieve their potential. The result of our current practice is a figurative "glass ceiling" for those with ability, and it is unfair, unjust, and unwise.

The key points made in this chapter are:

- There is a barrier that keeps high-achieving students from realizing their academic potential, and it is another one of the serious negative effects of our current practice of single-date entry, twelve-month cohorts.

- Decelerating students on the basis of their achievement is six times more frequent than acceleration.
- Many children travel through their school programs always experiencing the threshold of success but not the high degree of success necessary for getting into more invigorating career-oriented programs.
- The significant numbers of students who are struggling to keep pace with curriculum expectations are constantly pulling down the level of classroom instruction so that expectations for the grade are not met.
- Our brightest and best are being reined in and held back by a "glass ceiling" that mitigates against them achieving their potential.
- Younger students are unable to overcome the deficit they had when they enrolled.
- Efforts to achieve the imperative of improving achievement for the weaker students, who are mostly younger students, interferes with the achievement of stronger, mostly older students.

10

Social Promotion

MASKING THE PROBLEM

Social promotion has already been referenced on several occasions because of its endemic and injurious presence in the education system. Even though there is little assessment of its impact, studies on student achievement require a reference to the role it plays. When educators use age, not academic achievement, to group students and to produce cohorts, it becomes essential that we understand the issues created in this phenomenon.

In order to assess social promotion and its relationship to the current practice of organizing students into age-based, single-date-entry cohorts, it is helpful to look at the context which gives rise to the system. Adults establish schools and the entire educational superstructure in which they operate. Their memory of childhood and the experience of life arguably make them suitable architects of a world in which they no longer live.

Collective memories of an agrarian past leave society as a whole influenced by the movements of the earth and sun, which require slightly more than 365 days to complete an endless cycle of life and death. This pattern is so ingrained in us that we continue unthinkingly to orient ourselves to nature's rhythms. This leaves us with a calendar year, an annual birthday, a marriage anniversary, an annual medical examination, and so on. Time appears to accelerate as we age to the point where a year measures very little, but it remains the primary shaper of routine and practice in our lives.

Therefore, for rule makers in our society it is logical to think in terms of years because adherence to an annual calendar of some sort reflects an embracing of the cultural norm. Human beings have lived this way for millennia, dating back to the earliest moments of recorded history in the ancient cultures along the great rivers of Egypt, Mesopotamia, India, and China. Contrarian thinking is not something people readily adopt. Nevertheless, this is precisely what must happen, if we are to address the core issue identified in this book.

Detached rule makers may downplay the disadvantage by stating that the differences are inconsequential and easily overcome. Some might go as far as to say, "Life is not fair anyway," or that "Given our fiscal limitations, a twelve-month, single-date-entry system is the best we can do." Others might argue that "It worked well for our parents and for us, so it is good enough for our children too."

But the educational system today is not the same as it was for our grandparents or for the parents who are currently raising children. Rules such as entry date have remained the same, but the practices in our schools have changed. For example, when educators began to face universal participation, they initially failed students who fell behind their grade placement. An article in one of Canada's national newspapers, the *Globe and Mail* (June 9, 2007) touched on this issue. Writing about the experiences of the Edmonton public school district, the article stated:

> The realization crept up on Edmonton school administrators and shocked them to the core: One in five children was failing Grade 1. It was the early 1980s and officials learned of the high retention rate by chance through a testing program that found that about 20 per cent of pupils, many of them boys whose birthdays fell just before the enrolment cutoff, were in their second year of Grade 1.

Failing students certainly was common in those days, and birth month, especially for boys, was a significant factor.

The newspaper article went on to explain that by 2007, across Canada, holding children back has become increasingly rare. Instead, children who failed to meet minimum grade standards usually moved ahead with their peers. This is the practice we refer to as social promotion. It arose out of well-intentioned compassion for children who were thought to acquire poor self-esteem if they were held back. Studies seemed to suggest that students would be more successful in school if they remained with age-level peers.

The article indicated, however, that among teachers, there is dissent about the merits of social promotion, with some seeing the practice as ineffective in addressing gaps in learning. What is more, the research is taking a different perspective as new information comes to light. It is not my intention to review the findings, which are readily available elsewhere, because this book is not about the merits of social promotion.

Consequently, my focus is on social promotion's impact on the data related to relative-age effect and the masking effect it has on the truth of student achievement. As long as parents remain confused about the negative consequences of social promotion in regard to age and achievement, there is little likelihood that genuine reform will take place.

Stories Demonstrate How the Problem Is Masked

During the focus group sessions undertaken while writing this book, parents became aware of the data record found in this book and were justifiably upset. They commented that teachers virtually refused to hold a student back because it would damage self-esteem. Parents noted that their child would come home at the end of the school year and blurt out, "I passed!" even though the parents were aware this was not really the case. Because this story is repeated so often to so many parents, the public becomes desensitized to what they believe is the new norm.

Teachers, who were also part of a focus group, had a mixed reaction to the data on social promotion. Some expressed concern with the thought that social promotion would solve self-esteem issues. Others pointed out that students know who can and cannot read well, and that self-esteem is formed in these real-life contexts, not in retention or promotion. It is unrealistic to many teachers that students are not aware of their relative standing and, then, that this knowledge deters the student from having confidence in their efforts at success.

A grade one teacher expressed her opinion by referencing a student who did not want to come to school because he knew he was not as successful as his friends. The teacher went on to say the boy was born near the end of the registration window. Therefore, she felt a moral imperative draw her toward this struggling student because she knew that stronger students in the classroom bond socially and shun weaker students. She expressed a deep, personal need to make sure that the needs of lower-end students were not forgotten because this is the most important need in teaching.

Therefore she acknowledged feeling pressure to adapt the curriculum to meet students' needs, that is, to adjust downward her expectations for the curriculum, classroom activities, and homework. Put in the colloquial language of the day, it was her responsibility to "dumb down" the learning environment to a point where the slowest students experienced success. Educators usually find the term "dumb down" offensive and understandably so. Its use promotes a negative perception of teaching. The previous chapter, however, provides evidence regarding how the educational needs of our brightest and best students are secondary to the needs of those benefiting from the moral imperative.

The teachers in the focus group referenced another pressure related to social promotion. They indicated they understood that parents feel peer pressure regarding the progress of their child. In fact, teachers feel pressure from many parents who want more and faster learning to occur. If parents hear bad news about their child's lack of success, they then take it personally and seek to attribute blame. Sometimes parents take out their frustration on their children, thereby making the problem more acute.

Consequently, teachers are reticent to be the bearers of bad news. As a result, parents remain ignorant of the situation and the relationship between the teacher, the school, and the parents remains cordial and artificially productive. If the issue was simply one of producing a consumer product or of providing a nonessential service, the lack of transparency would still be wrong, but the consequences would not be so tragic. The lines of communication between teachers and parents needs to be open and characterized by informed integrity. Why? One superintendent explained it this way: we need to change the system because the system is supposed to be here to serve the kids.

Another administrator stated that he did not feel there were many in the public, including parents, who would be able to understand that many children were functioning below grade level. He was referencing a problem he saw among parents of middle school students, and his concern was that they would soon be arriving at the high school where he was the principal, and where teachers placed greater emphasis on teaching prescribed curricular content than on adapting content for significant variations in student ability.

Unless a school system has undertaken the arduous process of articulating standards for its curriculum, a relatively common approach in secondary schools is to segregate students by ability and then apply the bell curve to assess academic progress. Unfortunately, this assessment practice only serves to mislead everyone regarding the true achievement of the learner and, again, hide from public view a true description of learning.

One parent in our focus group related a poignant story of how the social promotion system almost led to a disastrous result for her son. "For many years," she said, "we were misled into believing our son was doing fine in school." When he was in grade nine, his classroom teacher told us he was functioning at a grade five level. The parent then explained that it took her some time to get over the shock of this revelation, but when she did she spared no expense in acquiring costly compensatory programming for him to bring him back to grade level.

Once he enrolled in university and experienced success there, she felt sufficiently confident about what had happened and what needed to be done to share her experience with other parents. Her goal, she said, was "to ensure parents would be sensitized to the lack of transparency that is in the school system."

Many school administrators today are willing to acknowledge that their schools' efforts to meet the moral imperative are disadvantaging stronger students. In their focus groups, these educational leaders described situations where the stronger students were "spinning their wheels" because teachers are so focused on meeting the needs of weaker students that they did not have the time and the energy to address the needs of stronger students. This led to comments that students experiencing behavioral problems were bright students who were not having their needs met. In the colorful language of one principal's metaphor, "Stronger students are nails that stand up; teachers hammer them down, resulting in rebellion."

School district trustees were the last group to address this issue, and they, too, expressed a similar perspective on the impact social promotion was having on the academically stronger students. It was their perception that these students were not getting the attention they required to stretch and challenge them in accordance with their ability. However, while they were on the topic of social promotion, some trustees digressed to make the point that they were hearing disgruntled voices in the community who wanted the district to discontinue its practice of promoting students who fell even further behind their age peers. The trustees concurred that a newer attitude was emerging that this ongoing practice should not continue.

The trustees were sympathetic about the problems a change like this would bring, and they recognized that teachers "don't like to hold kids back" and, therefore, stopping this longtime practice was going to require massive reeducation in the system. These trustees, then, could easily see how a current emphasis on the weak students was a deterrent to academically strong students who would have achieved their potential if the teachers had provided them with their "fair share" of time, resources, and support.

In summary, many academically weak students are annually promoted with their social group. A disproportionate number are born in the latter half of the registration period. The current model of an annual, single-date-entry system, combined with the relative-age effect, is putting these later-birth-month students on a treadmill that does not allow sufficient time for them to catch up. These students fall further and further behind while realizing self-fulfilled prophesies that they are not able to experience academic success.

Yes, they sometimes are retained a grade in schools where retention remains an option; however, in many other schools these students pass through the grade levels on a marginal basis, leaving the schools faced with ever-increasing pressure to throw more scarce resources at the problem. At the same time, these expensive efforts force academically stronger students to cope with the glass ceiling effect, which essentially suppresses their desire to work with diligence and enthusiasm to achieve their best. Consequently, social promotion has negatively impacted both our strong and weak students.

The key points made in this chapter are:

- Failing students was common a few decades ago, and birth month, especially for boys, was a significant factor.
- More recently, children who failed to meet minimum grade standards usually moved ahead with their peers in a practice known as "social promotion."
- Teachers feel a pressure to "dumb down" the learning environment to a point where the slowest students experience success.
- Students are passing through the grade levels on a marginal basis, leaving the schools faced with ever-increasing pressure to throw more scarce resources at the problem.
- Social promotion has negatively impacted both our strong and weak students.

A Global Perspective

NORWAY CONFIRMS THE DISADVANTAGE

Even though relative-age effect has been identified and named as an educational issue, extensive studies utilizing large-scale populations are few in number. Norway is one other large educational jurisdiction that has examined the relative-age effect, which makes it a viable system for comparison purposes when examining the issues identified in this book. Strom (2004) summarized his findings of Norway's education system, including a quantitative analysis of the long-term effect of birth month and student achievement in that country.

Consistency over time is an essential element in procuring quality data in educational research. Strom points out in his report that the Norwegian school system employs a set of practices that make it easy to generate high-level statistical data. This means that his findings are easy to interpret. His focus was on student achievement for fifteen- to sixteen-year-old students in Norway using international achievement tests in reading from the Organization for Economic Cooperation and Development (OECD).

These tests, which are known as the Programme for International Student Assessment (PISA), are used in many countries, but are reliable in Norway because the country adheres so closely to a set of strict rules. For example, Norway mandates:

1. Strict enrollment rules require every child born in a certain calendar year to begin school at the same point in time.
2. Students are almost never retained in a grade or promoted faster than the normal rule.
3. Public schools use a national curriculum for all students.
4. National rules are in place pertaining to maximum class size, criteria for special education, and teacher certification.
5. All students start school in mid-August, and the school year lasts until mid-June.

These rules facilitated an effective study because, with very few exceptions, all Norwegian students had been in school for an identical length of time during a one-year range. Further, students being tested had been exposed to the curriculum for exactly the same number of months. Given these clear parameters, achievement levels can be easily correlated with the age of the student.

In many other countries, and certainly in Canada and the United States, the rules are less rigid; consequently, researchers often have to nuance the conclusions. For example, there is usually greater freedom to choose the year in which their child will enter the system. In the region of my major study, children had to register for grade one if they reached the age of six by September. Children born after September had the opportunity to enroll in the following September, although few ever exercised this option.

There is relative consistency across North America for determining rules surrounding the appropriate age for enrollment into grade one. Generally the beginning ages vary by only a few months. However, other countries employ a standard that is considerably different. In the Netherlands, for example, all children are required to enroll in the beginning of the academic year they turn five years old (Leuven et al., 2003). Around the world, therefore, there are varying perspectives regarding when a child is sufficiently mature for experiencing success, and unlike in Norway, the length of time students have been in school is not constant within a one-year time frame.

Variation in achievement, as Strom indicates, "Reflects both variances in age, variations in school length and potential variations in parents' propensity to delay or accelerate school start for their children." This variegated situation makes it difficult to assess the impact of age on achievement, except in countries like Norway where the cultural pattern of rigid entry makes it relatively easy to assess.

Strom summarizes his study by concluding that students from the last quarter of the birth year remain significantly disadvantaged relative to their older classmates for as long as they remain in school. In his words, "I find that the oldest students, born in January just after the school entry cut-off date, score nearly at one-fifth of a standard deviation higher than the youngest students born in December, just before the cut-off date." In order to make the meaning of this clear to the public, Strom referenced a statistic that is widely known and understood: "This age effect is approximately equal to the estimated effect from having (the student's) father with high education."

This Norwegian study is significant because it assesses a longer term impact of relative age on student achievement, while at the same time providing some strict controls for a number of variables which are known to impact learning. For example, Strom includes reasonably objective student background and family variables traditionally used in socioeconomic analyses associated with variances in student achievement.

Therefore, his analysis controlled for such important variables as gender, father's and mother's education, and labor market attachment (full-time workers), educational resources in the home, birth order, family size, and whether the student spoke a language other than Norwegian. In assessing student achievement against these many variables, Strom concludes that "The rigid enrollment rules in Norway imply that students born late in the year face a significant disadvantage compared to their older classmates."

One other aspect of Strom's research is particularly significant for our current purposes. Strom echoes my perception that researchers have paid relatively little attention to the relationship between educational outcomes and the age at which students are enrolled in school. In his review of the literature he found that researchers have focused on the early school years and mistakenly assumed that the ill effects of age on achievement disappear after the first few years as the experiences of life neutralize the harmful effects.

The Norwegian study, with its focus on fifteen- through sixteen-year-old students, provides convincing evidence that the effect remains and that it is statistically significant. The Norwegian study thus confirms my findings which were based on a large sample of students in Canada over many years.

The longitudinal nature and the use of universal populations in a school system combine to generate greater validity in the findings.

The findings in both Norway and Canada make clear a lingering negative effect for those who entered with birth dates later in the year, and my study sheds light on the fact that the negative effect for this group creates a negative effect for those born early in the year. Almost all children are disadvantaged in the current system, and scarce human and material resources are squandered.

THE WORLD'S CONSTANT PURSUIT FOR RESOLUTION

As already indicated, research on relative-age effect is rather minimal, but among the little that exists there is evidence that the older students in the one-year cohort experience higher levels of achievement than the younger ones in the cohort (Crosser, 1991; Sharp et al., 1994). These researchers concluded, however, that the effects are relatively small and decrease as the age cohort progresses through the education system.

While the effects of age within a twelve-month cohort are settled, there remains disagreement about the best age at which to begin formal education. Mayer and Knutsen (1999) found that younger children scored higher achievement on cognitive tests than did older children in the same age cohort. This finding, and others like it, supports the argument that parents should enroll their children at a younger age, but not at a younger age in a cohort of twelve months.

Some school systems in Europe have taken this to an extreme, and children are enrolled as early as age two. Considerable social pressure is then brought to bear on parents who choose to keep their children at home, even for a year or two. One Canadian mother living temporarily in a university city in Belgium, who claimed to speak for many other expatriates, related how international students were routinely belittled and scolded in public from the marketplace and grocery store to the doctor's office and public library because their young children were with them during the day and not enrolled in school.

They were thought to be disadvantaging their children, which in her case were two and four years old. This young mother indicated how, with her little children, she was rudely pushed aside at the pay register because folks were actually angry that she had not given her children over for others to train. Examples like this one reveal how some countries take early intervention to an extreme.

At the other end of the spectrum are educators such as Shepard and Smith (1986) who examined retention in a grade and found higher rates for children born near the end of the age cohort. A significant aspect in this study pertains to the matter of choice exercised by parents who made a strategic decision on the part of the child to delay entry into the education program because of concern that their child was too immature. Their study concluded that younger children enrolling in the school system experienced a higher retention rate.

These studies focused primarily on academic achievement. Others have looked at other domains and found the impact of early enrollment was negative. Goodman (2003), for example, found that the youngest in the age cohort experienced greater psychological disadvantage than their older peers.

Byrd, Weitzman, and Auinger (1997) reviewed parental reports on behavior problems from a national representative sample of children aged seven to seventeen who participated in the United States' Child Health Supplement of the 1988 National Health Interview survey. In this study, old-for-grade students (who had not been retained) were more likely to score high in behavior problems than other (nonretained) children, but this age-of-entry effect increased with age. The negative effects became particularly apparent during adolescence. In one way, this finding made perfect sense. Older students were bored in their school program because too much attention was given to the weaker students, and their boredom was manifesting itself in negative behavior.

Goodman, Gledhill, and Ford (2003) undertook a similar study in the United Kingdom with children aged five to fifteen and found virtually the opposite result. Strom's response to this apparent contradiction is that Goodman, Gledhill, and Ford's study relied on an inappropriately small sample that does not allow a generalization to the broader public. By working with such a small group it was not possible for the researchers to take into account how parents exercised their option to voluntarily retain their young children for a school year so that they would be in the older portion of the next school age cohort.

Cascio and Schanzenbach (2008) reported on how American parents were increasingly delaying their child's entry to the first grade to the extent that six-year-old enrollment declined from 96 percent in 1968 to 84 percent in 2005. Deming and Dynarski (2008) studied this finding and concluded that approximately two-thirds of this decline is the result of kindergarten teachers expressing concern about specific students' maturity levels for success in grade one as well as parents simply opting to delay their child's entrance into school—a practice known as "redshirting."

These authors also understood the deleterious effect on the young, immature learner when the school tracked or "streamed" them in the classroom. In this scenario children are routinely tracked on a set of criteria to see how they are performing. The problem is that the elements that are tracked become self-fulfilling prophecies. If it is "known" that younger children do not do as well as older children and age is tracked by the teachers, the teacher will find this preconception to be true.

Mashburn and Pianta's (2006) research determined that age of entry can trigger a set of teacher beliefs, classroom practices, and placement decisions that reflect interactional and transactional mechanisms. Consequently, schools would be well advised not to stream students into "groups" or to track them on predetermined factors of success.

This chapter demonstrates how few major studies there are on the subject of student achievement and birth month. When researchers have conducted them, there is confirmation that relative-age effect has a negative, long-term impact on students. One of this book's contributions to the literature is its publication of data linking the issue of an annual, single-date entry with the practice of grouping children into twelve-month groups.

The key points made in this chapter are:

- The Norwegian school system employs a pattern of rigid entry that makes it easy to generate high-level statistical data regarding the impact of relative-age effect.
- Students from the last quarter of the birth year remain significantly disadvantaged relative to their older classmates for as long as they remain in school.
- To date, researchers have paid relatively little attention to the relationship between educational outcomes and the age at which students are enrolled in school.
- Researchers have focused on the early school years and mistakenly assumed that the ill effects of age on achievement disappear after the first few years as the experiences of life neutralize the harmful effects.

The Finnish Solution:
Less Is More

FINLAND HAS A BETTER IDEA

Of the many options available for dealing with the handicapping of students evident in the relative-age effect, the model utilized in Finland likely has the least appeal for North Americans. Finland and Canada are both high achievers on the international tests conducted by the Organization for Economic Cooperation and Development (OECD) and known as Programme for International Student Assessment (PISA). Therefore it is essential that these countries be included in any analysis of educational effectiveness (Canadian provinces are all considered a country in PISA because they oversample their student population during testing).

Canadian rules of student engagement are fairly representative of many regions in the world, but Finland, as well as a few other countries in that geographical region, is different because of their school-starting age of seven years. Waiting an additional year before beginning formal education is a significant difference, especially when we recognize that one year in the life of a six-year-old represents 16 percent of their lifespan. Varying educational processes in human development at this age have profound measurable effects.

Certainly there are many contextual variables in Finland which are helpful in achieving high educational success. The country is comparatively unicultural, as evidenced by the fact that 84 percent of Finns belong to the same church. Also, immigration is relatively low at less than 1 percent annually. With so few foreigners entering the country, language differences are minimal. North American educators understand the significance when language barriers are not involved during classroom instruction.

Furthermore, the preference for a socialistic approach to political, social, and economic organization has created a situation where the gap between rich and poor is relatively small. Consequently, socioeconomic variables, which tend to create significant differences in countries more oriented to free-enterprise individualism, are relatively less likely to create differentiation in achievement. This aspect, too, is certainly different from what is evident in North America, where variances in socioeconomic status explain approximately half of the variance in student achievement, with the other half explained by variances in the quality of educational services provided by the school.

While these social factors are significant in explaining a portion of Finland's success in education, the value that the Finns place on education also must be acknowledged. Barber and Mourshed, in the 2007 McKinsey Report, provide information on teacher salaries and where Finland's teachers stand relative to other OECD countries. Based on percent of GDP per capita, Finland's education system front-ends teacher salaries so that they are comparable with those in other OECD countries. They then lose ground to OECD countries thereafter, and fall considerably behind at the maximum end of the pay scale.

Therefore, the salary grid for teachers in Finland does not make the case that teachers are particularly valued, at least when salaries are taken to reflect what society really values. Barber and Mourshed go on to illustrate a different way of ascertaining value by indicating that teachers are only able to give the talent that they possess and, therefore, a measure of value is evident in who is ultimately selected into the teaching profession.

Teacher Talent Really Matters

According to these authors, the top-performing systems recruit the top school-system graduates. In South Korea, the top 5 percent of high school graduates apply; in Finland it is the top 10 percent; in Singapore and Hong Kong it is the top 30 percent; but in United States applicants into teaching are generally from the bottom third. Not only do Finland's high school graduates place great value in joining the teaching profession, but the teacher-training institutions then add importance to the profession by accepting only 10 percent of the applicants. In Finland, then, teaching is a highly valued occupation where "stars" are at work.

However, reviews of Finland's educational success frequently disregard some data which immediately raises eyebrows. Many people assume that the time a student is in school receiving instruction is directly related to success in student achievement, just as it is believed that spending more in education increases student learning. Neither is true, however (Barber, 2008)! In Finland's case, rules for engaging students in educational activities certainly demonstrates that time, by itself, is not highly correlated with success.

The chart below in figure 12.1, compiled in 2005 by the Council of Ministers of Education in Canada (CMEC), demonstrates that Finland's students aged seven through fourteen spend the least amount of instructional time in school. Their student achievement results, however, were the highest in the world on the 2006 PISA tests. Indeed, Finland is consistently one of the highest-achieving education systems in the world.

The United States and Canada are missing from the chart because the data is difficult to gather in these two countries, which do not have a centralized national governance model in education. Both countries have constitutions that place education as the responsibility of the states and provinces. Therefore, there is not a consistent rule across the country about time spent in school or instructional hours. Overall, because these two countries are so

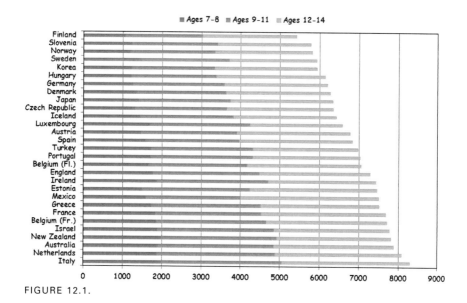

FIGURE 12.1.

similar in their educational structures and practices, children end up spending approximately as much time in school as France does.

Less Can be More

This graph certainly raises many questions but contains a powerful message about educating children. Simply stated, less is more! In Finland, children do not begin grade one until the age of seven, whereas most countries in the world begin at least a year earlier, or even several years earlier. There are a few countries, such as Estonia, which is listed, and Russia, which is not listed, that follow the Finnish registration pattern.

As stated previously, intellectual maturation is significant in the early years of a child's life, and delaying the onset of formal schooling by a year provides opportunity for many more children to reach the stage that is necessary for academic success. Since Finland and a few other countries in that region of the world do not begin formal schooling until age seven, the chart begins with that age in order to provide a consistent measure of instructional time in all countries for the period of time that children from all countries listed are in attendance.

If the chart began at age six, Finland's bar line would be considerably shorter than it already is relative to most of the other countries. Finland would add "zero" to the total, whereas most of the other countries would be adding close to 1,000 hours more instruction. Finland is truly one of the amazing enigmas in the ongoing debates about time on learning in educational reform.

Figure 12.1 tells a truly incredible story. Given the fact that the PISA tests are an age-based test and that all students writing the test are fifteen years old, it means that students in Finland will have had at least one year less of school than their peer group in most other countries. Eventually they go through twelve grades, but they finish one year later than do students in most of the world. Their education system with a delayed entry results in a delayed exit.

In North America, students writing the PISA are usually in grade nine when the testing program is administered in March. Students in Finland are only in grade eight; yet their overall student achievement scores are at the highest level relative to the rest of the world. In some respects their achievement level is simply profound yet profoundly simple. Their advantages with a unicultural society and commitment to education is, in this author's view, supported by a rule related to the age that students begin formal learning.

While Finns have only been in school for approximately 5,400 hours from age seven (i.e., including grade one) through age fourteen, French and North American students will have received approximately 7,600 hours after grade one, that is, not counting the hours they had in grade one. Stated differently, students in France and North America spend approximately 40 percent more time in school from age seven through fourteen. Including the additional year in grade one that begins at the age of six, France and North America spend more than 50 percent more time in school compared to their counterparts in Finland by the time they write the PISA tests at age fifteen. This is profound evidence that less can be more!

Finland's strategy of delaying entry into formal learning for up to one year allows a larger percent of students to begin formal learning when they are developmentally ready and more mature. Such a rule makes much more sense in helping students achieve their potential than the many costly efforts of bringing students into preschool programs at earlier ages. It also reduces the need for costly expenditures for remediation programs and facilitates maximizing instructional time for students developmentally ready to learn. If the well-being of the child was not reason enough to adopt such a practice—and it is—the economic justification is clear: you get more "bang for the buck" if you delay children until they are mature enough to take advantage of the learning experience schools provide.

However, the cultural shift that would need to take place for age seven to be adopted in North America as the appropriate age to begin school is seemingly too great to be considered realistic. Reason, based on data, is irrelevant in the minds of many because this has been absent in education for too long. Added to this reticence to change, based on tradition and habit, is a public skepticism about research in the social sciences, a wish to have children in custodial care so that parents can get on with careers, and a desire to see children "race to the top" by queuing up early at the starting gate, that is, grade one.

In spite of all these societal obstacles, we must still make the case for consideration of the Finnish model. Their decision to delay entry until seven years of age has the effect of giving all children one more year to mature, thus closing the gap between January- and December-born children. Their approach effectively neutralizes the relative-age effect, because it ensures that almost all children are sufficiently mature to handle formal learning.

Even if their approach was not adopted by society as a whole, it should be offered as a reasonable alternative for schools and parents, thus giving our North American system a creative way to help more students achieve their potential. The end result would be a stronger, more equitable school system, which we could only see as a positive development.

The key points made in this chapter are:

- Finland's students demonstrate high levels of student achievement.
- Finland is different from North American practices because of their school-starting age of seven years.
- Finland's education system also benefits from a unicultural environment and their capacity to recruit top school-system graduates.
- Finland's strategy of delaying entry into formal learning for up to one year allows a larger percent of students to begin formal learning when they are developmentally ready and more mature.
- North American students spend more than 50 percent more time in school compared to their counterparts in Finland by the time they write the PISA tests at age fifteen.
- Less can be more if we wait for more students to be sufficiently mature for formal learning.

13

The New Zealander's Solution

It is almost a universal practice for children from a twelve-month period of time to begin their schooling on the same day. This particular day is often referred to as the first day of the school year. Throughout this book we refer to this as the first day of the annual single-date-entry system. While most school systems have their first day of school near the beginning of September, some begin in August in order to divide the school year into equal parts when punctuated by the Christmas break.

New Zealand stands out as an exception to the single-date-entry rule: it has its students begin school at various times throughout the school year. The first day of a student's birth month becomes the month for registration. Conversations with educators in New Zealand indicate that they actually find it strange that all students would enter school on a single common date in the calendar, as occurs throughout the rest of the world.

New Zealand's approach requires more time and effort to implement, which goes a long way to explaining why other countries have not adopted it. Once teachers become accustomed to the ongoing intake of new registrants, the procedures are routinized and the additional work is minimal. Grade one classes begin the year with lower numbers in anticipation of an influx of students later in the year. In other words, classroom seats are reserved for students who will enter later. The result is that teachers are able to respond to the individual needs.

A significant rule in this approach pertains to the exit process, where the expectation is that students will complete their elementary school program at a common time for entry into the next level of schools. Therefore elementary-age students are either being accelerated or decelerated in their educational progress to accommodate an exit consistent with the commencement of the next level of schooling. While there are multiple entry points during the year, there is only one exit point.

There appears to be little financial savings in this method. Indeed, it is likely more costly because the government is required to provide funding to save spaces for students who will enter partway through the year. The teacher workload is somewhat reduced in the first year, as teachers work with a reduced number of students for part of the year. The workload is further reduced by the fact that when students enter, they are relatively more mature than is the case in a single-date-entry system.

A PISA 2003 international test analysis (Sprietsma, 2007), found that New Zealand's students at age fifteen had approximately an equal percentage of students who were one grade level behind or ahead. Twenty other countries participated in this study. Those which used aggressive acceleration and deceleration strategies, such as Canada and the United States, found that the percentage of decelerations was much higher than the percentage of accelerations. In Canada, for example, the ratio of deceleration to acceleration was approximately 17:1. This demonstrates how a focus on weak students (mostly from the latter birth months) suppressed the achievement of stronger ones.

New Zealand's model for introducing students into formal schooling always elicited a positive response during focus group discussions. The fact that government reserves seats in the grade one classroom for students having their sixth birthday during the school year was particularly appealing. Delaying the entry into formal learning until the child was six years of age was also considered a strength in this approach.

The key point made in this chapter is:

- New Zealand's approach to readiness has children beginning grade one in the month a child turns six.

Getting Down to "Brass Tacks"

ALL TEACHERS ARE NOT EQUAL

The solutions found in Finland and New Zealand are instructive to larger countries whose educational environments are more complex. The key is to find which principles are transferable to a larger population, and which are ideal for the idiosyncratic situations these smaller countries face. One aspect of the educational environment that all countries share is the relationship between the student and the teacher, which is the subject of this chapter.

We have considered a number of unfair practices in our school systems that leave a lifelong legacy of poor self-esteem and substandard achievement. Among these were the single-date entry into school, the twelve-month span for a grade cohort, a tendency to bias in grading, and a philosophically unsound approach to retention and promotion. The negative aspects of these oft-debated issues are connected in subtle but real and harmful ways. It is time now to enter the classroom and look at the day-to-day life of the child in relationship to his or her teacher. Here we find yet another common practice that results in unfairness and disadvantage.

During a lengthy career in education it was my privilege to visit more than 20,000 classrooms. There were huge variances in classroom practices as well as in teaching capacity. One particularly noteworthy and bothersome observation was that professional development programs had little impact on teachers. Whereas some were quick to explore and implement innovative reforms, a large percent persisted in teaching the way they had taught regardless of the corrective or helpful information they received. It became apparent that professional development only enjoyed an enduring beneficial effect across a school if the administrators became involved and worked directly with teachers.

As a system administrator, it was difficult for me to express these perceptions publicly because defensive behaviors immediately surfaced. When one deals with a thousand teachers in a system, the relationship inevitably becomes impersonal, so that no matter how well-meaning, sympathetic, and sincere a statement may be, it comes across as critical and negative. New ideas and helpful suggestions can be rejected out of hand by the group in such an environment of distrust, even though as individuals they would express eagerness to improve. As a consequence, implementing change took a great deal of time, even if it appeared modest and intuitive.

At the outset of my teaching career, a school administrator introduced me to Benjamin Bloom's concept of mastery learning. While undertaking the myriad of tasks faced by new teachers, effort was immediately launched into developing individualized learning modules for my students subsequently borrowed by many other teachers. The thrill associated was immediately evident. As a consequence, a number of colleagues saw the results and implemented the modules in their classrooms. Developing these programs required hundreds of hours of work beyond the normal workload, but the high level of job satisfaction that resulted ameliorated the tedium of long nights and short weekends.

Students who participated in the program accelerated at such a pace that teachers of older students, who would soon inherit mine, began to criticize and find fault. They were concerned because parents were beginning to draw the comparisons to their work with students. At times it was emotional. Some parents who attended parent-teacher conferences literally broke down and wept because they had never seen their child so motivated. Students pleaded to remain after school so they could spend additional time working with the resources. Not all teachers were displeased: some liked that fact that forty-five students were in my class so that their class sizes were correspondingly reduced.

Subsequently, as a school district superintendent making 400 school visits per year, principals were routinely asked about their teachers' talent and with which teachers they would not place their own child. The result of that informal research revealed that principals would not place their own child in 17 percent of their school's classrooms. If a classroom was like a fast-food restaurant which could be visited or avoided as desired, such a statistic would be inconsequential; however, as President Obama explained it to the US Chamber of Commerce (March 1, 2010), "Our kids get only one chance at an education and we need to get it right."

Many students experience teaching that provides them with an advantage or disadvantage. The environment the teacher creates is not neutral, and not mechanical. In other words, some teachers have the ability to help their students achieve more than just an expected "year's worth" of learning, others do not. Some educators explain away these differences in achieving student success by saying that "the good and the bad equal out over time."

This type of statement should be considered in the context of how much the education system is rooted in a factory model. In a factory setting, widgets arrive at a stage where they are approved to a certain level of certification. Basically they are all very similar and ready to be used in a product designed for them. In this process, defective products are summarily removed as the assembly line continues.

Some people see teacher preparation fitting this metaphor (Weisberg et al., 2009). Teachers are likened to be on an assembly line where deficient persons are removed as the assembly line continues. Those remaining and proceeding on the line are assessed as being sufficiently equal and interchangeable. Such an assessment is not reality! There are substantial differences between teachers, and the public has the right to expect constant, energetic remediation if not diligent dismissal.

Weakness Needs to be Weeded Out

Teacher competence is a sensitive issue and is raised because educational leadership has not been very diligent in weeding out poor performers or achieving change in weak classroom teachers. With so many students captured within the relative-age-effect phenomenon, their plight is exacerbated when they are also placed in classrooms with lower-quality teachers. Therefore, it is possible that children born near the end of the registration year face double jeopardy when they also are placed with teachers who are unable to support student achievement gains of at least one year.

Similarly, students at the other end of the spectrum and appropriately labeled as "high fliers" may actually achieve one grade level with a weak teacher, but their actual gain is less than expected. In effect, these stronger students experience the glass ceiling effect because their weaker teacher is unable to adequately address their capacity for achieving higher learning gains. They have progressed, but a potential for accelerated challenge and learning is not addressed.

Reforming teacher competency is a slow and arduous process. The process can result in confrontation when low-performing teachers are too slow in adopting changes which will make them more effective in the classroom or, worse, unable to meet the acceptable threshold. McGrath (2007) summarizes the extent of the problem:

> For more than 20 years, we have been gathering the responses of 150,000-plus school site administrators to our anecdotal survey regarding the performance of school district teachers, and their evaluations. We have found, according to those administrator responses, that between three percent and five percent of permanent teachers are functioning in the lowest category of "poor." Another thirteen percent to twenty percent need improvement to meet satisfactory performance and can be considered marginal.

She goes on to state that the "problem is that most administrators think that feedback within the supervisory process is the same as discipline. It is not."

McGrath's assessment is supported by many other researchers. *Macleans* magazine also reviewed this educational issue in a feature story dated July 8, 2009. Barry Bennett, a researcher from the Ontario Institute for Studies in Education, provided his perspective which poignantly summarizes the end result of the problem: "the dismissal process is so onerous, the risk of reprisal from teachers' unions so great, that most principals find it's not worth the effort." The writer of the article, Rachel Mendleson, went on to say that instead of dismissal, school boards "approve transfers, or hide struggling teachers where their deficiencies can go unnoticed. The result however, is this: a system that keeps incompetent teachers in the classroom."

Perhaps out of frustration with such slow progress in both removing and strengthening/helping weak teachers, the education system is focused on changing system practices or policies, such as timetabling, hours of instruction, school calendars, instructional groupings, and class size. Changing the rules of engagement in schools is usually less stressful than dealing with personnel issues, which are frequently associated with interpersonal conflict.

While the ideal would be to address the failure of teachers to embrace professional development, there is value in pursuing the easier or at least less personally stressful path of changing rules, because rules, too, create serious handicaps for students. For example, a change in our "rules" would allow us to discard the lockstep approach to education that forces stronger academic students to wait for slower peers to acquire sufficient knowledge or skill to catch up.

Many classroom teachers want to free their students from the lockstep movement through the school system which is associated with strict adherence to the "grade equals age" concept. Accomplishing this freedom requires individualized programming, also known as personalized learning, that allows a student to progress at his/her own pace while receiving the requisite instruction at the precise moment when it is necessary for their ongoing success.

Establishing the correct pace in learning is highly advantageous from a motivational standpoint because it leaves students simultaneously confident in their capacity to learn, while generating challenges that inspire effort without undue fear of failure. An improper pace that "throttles" them back is demotivational and produces disengagement from school.

In the large, twelve-year kindergarten to grade nine study we undertook in our region, we surveyed students and asked specifically about their levels of satisfaction with classroom practices. They responded negatively about their lack of engagement with their teachers and their classroom activities. So unequivocal were they in their negative feeling, we drew the conclusion that the lack of meaningful engagement was endemic in our system.

Disengagement is not just a factor of poor teacher-student rapport, which is why rule changes are important. It also arises indirectly from the slavish way in which we adhere to the idea that every child is to progress one grade level per year. Our society has debated the merits of this system for decades, but little change will occur as long as the education system is not forced to number among its priorities a financially positive bottom line. Furthermore, our school systems rarely measure annual achievement gains. The Race to the Top initiative in the United States is a significant effort aimed at measuring annual achievement gains.

THERE ARE FINANCIAL BENEFITS IN THE FINNISH MODEL

Helping school districts come to grips with the economic impact of their decisions is difficult. From the student's perspective, retention is a momentous affair. It occurs most frequently in the early grades when one year is a substantial portion of a child's life. Dealing in year-long increments is a serious matter. It would be much easier for the child if the increment was smaller, but our grade structure is rigidly confined to a twelve-month calendar, and the mindset within the education system is dominated by a commitment to begin a new grade during the first month of the school year.

What we need is a dramatically different approach which allows teachers to personalize learning—something they find difficult to do given our current practice of acceleration and deceleration. We have already clarified that implementing the Finnish model for North American society is unreasonable. Delaying entry into formal education by a full year until the child is seven years of age is a difficult challenge for working parents who require custodial care for their preschool children. Delaying school until a child reached seven would cause parents to turn to the state for taxpayer-funded child care.

From a strictly financial perspective, taxpayers might welcome the change, as it would actually reduce costs with the release of approximately one-twelfth of the classroom teachers. For twelve consecutive years there would be only eleven grades operating in the school system. The later entry age potentially increases readiness for learning, therefore enabling greater student success. This success reduces the need for costly remedial programs to assist the large percent of students struggling academically within the current system.

Fewer teachers would also mean fewer administrative support staff such as secretaries. For one generation of students (twelve years), the 8 percent reduction in student population would necessitate construction of fewer new schools. Fewer classroom spaces require less energy and maintenance costs, and there would be fewer custodians in schools. The list of incidental savings goes on. In short, it is quite possible that cost reductions in the education budget could save taxpayers well over 10 percent annually on their school tax bill for more than a decade.

But embracing the Finnish model would produce trauma for some within the system. Teachers made redundant would be the most obviously affected group. The challenges they face would alone bring into question the merits of the change, even though there would be a marked improvement in the success of students who would benefit from a one-year delay. In addition to redundant teachers, there would be many others who would object, although perhaps not publicly. Some of the objections would likely be a smokescreen for other, deeply held objections that for one reason or another cannot be stated openly.

Some of these deeper issues could emerge from within the educational community not directly associated with the classroom. For example, fewer teachers in schools could impact principals' salaries downward because they frequently are paid according to the number of teachers they supervise. Even salaries of central office administrators could be pushed downward with the reduction in personnel. These are examples of pocketbook issues causing people within the system to have their judgment clouded by self-serving needs.

Teachers' union leaders could oppose the change because such a significant reduction in the workforce would immediately reduce the amount of funding they receive through union dues collected from teachers. These leaders, too, might experience a salary reduction or they might have to cut back on their services to their members. Of course, unions might react by raising dues to compensate for their loss of revenue which, in turn, could create opposition among otherwise neutral or supportive teachers.

These and other objections make it improbable that school systems in North America will opt for a shift in the age of entry from six to seven even though the delay holds the promise of improving success and saving money. Participants in focus groups find troublesome this latter aspect of saving money in education. They were impressed with the probability of improving student success, but they did not want the potential for savings to be a factor in decisions.

With these substantial savings, which could easily exceed 10 percent per annum, government could put into place publicly funded preschool programs to accommodate custodial-care needs of today's working families. Or, it could take some of the savings and implement a child credit program that would allow parents to determine how the savings would be allocated. Or, the savings could simply be returned to the taxpayer for a period of time until, once again, the school population would include twelve grades of students. Naturally, there are many more options that our political representatives and rule makers could choose/elect to consider.

What should not be lost in this scenario is the amazing thought that less cost would result in better education outcomes. One could only wish that there was political will to consider this worthy option. With reference to the Finnish model, it is apparent that more time in school does not necessarily correlate with success. Finnish children, who spend 50 percent less time in school by the time they write international tests at age fifteen, achieve at amazingly high levels, thus demonstrating that there is not a direct correlation between time in school and achievement. There is another, less-dramatic option. A system that has children enter school two times per year can have a substantial effect on student achievement and on their subsequent movement through the graded structure of the education system. In other words, a two-times-a-year entry system would be the elementary school's equivalent of the semester system which is widely used in secondary schools.

DUAL-ENTRY IS ANOTHER WAY

This second option, which we will refer to as the dual-entry system, would have children who are born in the six-month window from March 1 to August 31 begin school at the beginning of September. All students in this cohort would be six years old by their entry date in September. The next entry date would be for students born between September 1 and the end of the following February, who then would enter grade one on February 1.

In this second cohort, students born in February would commence grade one at five years and eleven months of age or older. This slight variation in ages between the two cohorts is necessitated by having ten months of school in a twelve-month calendar, where the summer vacation traditionally occurs in two consecutive months of July and August. Naturally this could also be altered if a school system chose to utilize a year-round education program.

In this dual-entry model, each cohort would then be in school for five consecutive months and, with one birth month's exception, have children begin formal learning when they are six years of age instead of what happens now in many school systems where children as young as five years and eight months can begin school in grade one. The effect would be to have a four-month delay for the youngest students currently entering grade one. Equally important is that the range in age of the students beginning grade one would only be six months and replace the annual single-date entry.

From an educational perspective, several major advantages occur with a dual-entry system. First, and probably foremost, the percentage of students achieving below grade level would be significantly reduced. Stated differently, there would be an immediate reduction in the percentage of failing students.

Indeed, the reduction would be dramatic. People find it difficult to understand this concept because the reduction in failure is so staggering.

As stated earlier in the large longitudinal study, December birth month retention rates were approximately 9 percent in kindergarten, another 9 percent in grade one, another 4 percent in grade two and so on, until by the end of grade nine 22 percent of December-born children had been retained at some point in their school career. December-birth-month students in the current system are in their fourth month of school after the beginning of the school year.

In a dual-entry system, where the December birth month would be compared to the fourth month of the current system, that is, April, retention rates would be negligible in kindergarten, 3 percent in grade one, another 1.5 percent in grade two and so on, with an aggregated retention of 9 percent at the end of grade nine. Therefore the overall decrease in student retention for the fourth birth month in a dual-entry system would be 13 percentage points, or approximately 60 percent fewer retained students.

Few people believe there are "silver bullets" in education, but this has to be as close to one as there is. Saving taxpayers a large sum of money while significantly improving educational outcomes is unheralded! Again, this data is only applicable to actual retentions. If teachers did not also employ social promotion, the percent of retained students currently traveling through our schools would certainly be higher.

Dual-Entry Improves Student Achievement

It is possible to show the impact of a dual-entry system using data from the longitudinal study. Figure 14.1 below depicts the number of grade three students who would have met the Acceptable Standard if the school year was

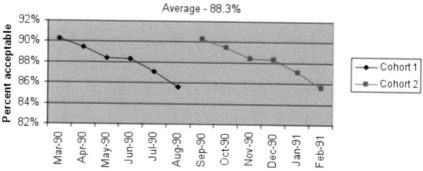

FIGURE 14.1.

comprised of two entry points. Students born in the second half of the current one-year cohort would be cut off from the bottom half of the line and would logically be expected to mirror achievement levels of the first-half cohort. Student achievement for the second half of the school year would immediately improve by 5 percent, which is a significant amount for a school system. Furthermore, it would create an impressive savings for the taxpayer.

Another benefit of a dual-entry approach for students and taxpayers is the reduction that would occur in the number of students teachers designate for remediation. Loss of self-esteem certainly occurs when students feel unsuccessful in their work, including when they are placed in remediation programs. This is especially true when the remedial efforts feature a pull-out strategy which is visible to peers.

The reasons for leaving the room on a regular basis to attend remedial sessions does not require a great deal of guesswork by the student or his/her peers, and the impact on self-esteem inevitably results in a self-fulfilling negative prophecy that the student is unable to learn as readily as others. These remedial programs are an added cost to the system because they require teacher services.

Another benefit which might occur in a dual-entry approach pertains to the pace of student progress in classrooms across the education system. Intuitively it seems that teachers would be more willing to accelerate or decelerate students when there is only one half of a year at issue rather than a full year. Dual entry does not eliminate entirely the "slave to the grade" mentality, but in the dual-entry system grades are replaced by levels where two levels equal one grade.

The impact of a decision to alter the progression of a student by half a year is not as consequential as a similar decision that involves a full year. Consequently, as the New Zealand model showed, teachers would more readily consider accelerating or decelerating grade placement by only one half year. As pointed out above, the New Zealand model demonstrated a far more equitable situation, with students being accelerated or decelerated in accordance with their academic progress.

The pace of student learning is currently a significant issue in educational reform. The lockstep, factory-type model requires reform, and a dual-entry system provides a reasonable, minimally invasive correction which could be embraced readily. It represents a directional change rather than a cataclysmic upheaval, which would be too difficult for a single generation of teachers to accept.

To make the change attractive and feasible, school systems would need to communicate clearly that children come first and that they are genuinely viewed as the most precious resource we have. They would also need to communicate that the current practice of introducing them into a system that is associated with a high degree of risk is unnecessary. Implementing educational change that reduces failure, raises learning achievement, and improves self-esteem communicates value for our children.

Instituting dual entry requires a cultural change within the teaching profession, because many schoolteachers are accustomed to working with the same class of students from the beginning of the school year to its conclusion. The semester system in high schools has already altered the perception that classes need to run for ten months, but the cultural shift has yet to impact the world of elementary education.

Today, the lengthy summer vacation constitutes and communicates a clear ending to the school year. This lengthy break from formal learning contributes to an incorrect public perception that students have reached a definite conclusion and a new beginning is soon to follow. Decades of practice have produced tradition and habit so that it is almost impossible to think of an elementary grade not beginning and ending for everyone, including the teacher, at the same time. Unless the school has a very small student population, they will not have the same teacher in September that they had when they "finished" in June.

In a dual-entry concept, June does not signal the end of a school year. Rather, it signals a break in formal learning time just like the traditional, albeit shorter, Christmas break. Usually students remain with the same teacher when they return after the Christmas break. Students entering grade one in February could remain with the same teacher after the summer break concluded and when school recommenced in September.

This preceding clarification is necessary because discussions with parents and teachers about the dual-entry concept reveal how enslaved to lockstep thinking our education culture has become. Fortunately school systems involved in school-year variations such as year-round education have considerable understanding of the neverending school year. In the adult world, most careers—especially those not associated with education—are unlikely to think of years where the beginning and ending is so significant.

This discussion is not intended to minimize the real possibility that a dual-entry initiative may require more-frequent class reorganizations. Dual entry implies organizational considerations two times per year, and reorganizations may be necessary even though not automatic. The semester system features two beginnings in a twelve-month period. Teachers may have different student populations as a result of these beginnings.

New Zealand, with its process of having students enter in their birth month, begins the school year with grade one classes having sufficient room to accommodate enrollment increases during the year. Similarly, governments which adopt a dual-entry concept can invest the savings from this initiative by reserving classroom seats to accommodate students arriving in the second entry. The following chapter demonstrates this potential.

Even when a strategy for saving seats is disregarded, problems associated with dual-entry reorganizations are not insurmountable. It is a well-established practice that the first few weeks of the school year are necessary to "restart the engines of learning" after the long summer break. A student's forgetting rate is as significant as is his or her learning rate. Technology is revolutionizing communication related to student progress so that teachers should not be requiring the traditional three weeks at the beginning of the school year to understand where their students may be academically. Student records are easily transmitted from the previous teacher to the one inheriting the new student.

Dual-Entry also Costs Less

When any initiative to improve education is introduced, the focus sooner or later is on the cost. There are few examples where the initiative does not have a price tag. Indeed, it is almost inconceivable that any improvement strategy would be a huge savings to taxpayers. Dual entry is truly a manifestation of "less is more." Just like the Finnish model with its start of formal learning at age seven, dual entry has savings that are instantaneous and cumulative.

The most obvious saving is accrued from having only one half of a class of grade one students entering in September. Therefore, in the first year of implementation, grade one would have approximately one half of the students registering at each entry point, which translates into a 2 percent savings for the school year (each grade represents one-twelfth of the budget for grades one through twelve education which approximates 8 percent of the budget).

In reality, the savings is more than 2 percent, but it is better to err on the conservative side rather than promise something that may mislead. Specifically, the savings would be greater because pupil-teacher ratios for class size are usually less for the initial years of schooling than they are for students in the older grades. To the extent that this is factual, savings for dual entry are projected to be greater than 2 percent of a school district's annual operating budget.

Since grade one would have one half of the student population in school for the full year and the other half would be in school for only half of the year, three-quarters of the 8 percent would be required for an annual savings of 2 percent for twelve consecutive years until the first dual exit from grade twelve occurred. In understanding this savings it is important to know that a full cohort of students is graduating and exiting from grade twelve every year. During this time period until a dual exit begins, grade one students are entering two times per year—hence the 2 percent savings annually for twelve years.

Huge additional savings are evident from establishing the dual-entry concept. Student retention in the current single-date-entry system is significant, and accommodating retained students for a longer period of time than the traditional twelve years requires more teachers, classrooms, and support staff such as caretakers, secretaries, and so on. Recall that one in six students was being retained an additional year in school and that the significant majority of these were victims of the single-date entry system. Dual entry greatly reduces the number of students requiring an additional year in school.

Furthermore, just as occurs when students enroll at age seven, much of the existing need for costly remediation programs is eliminated. In the annual single-date entry, the school system is attempting to achieve its moral imperative with so many students who are in need of remediation simply because of immaturity. Not only is there a savings in remedial teachers but also in their support services such as school psychologists—recall an observation from a focus group psychologist that almost all of his clients were last-quarter birth-month students. These combined savings are in addition to the 2 percent related to dual-entry funding mentioned above, and are also likely at least as much.

Improving educational success for students is what the education system is all about. Many people think that a measurement of improvement is based on how much money is spent. Spending is not an outcome. In education, money is an input. Student achievement is the outcome. My experience is that this kind of talk is an anathema. Suggestions that more can be achieved with less can produce considerable vehemence. Bringing about an improvement in student achievement by spending less money is a difficult concept to understand for many people, especially educators.

MAKING STUDENTS OUR FOCUS

This book is about placing the focus on what matters: student achievement and, ultimately, student success. The current practice of placing young children in twelve-month groupings by having an annual single-date-entry system is deleterious to student achievement. The group most disadvantaged by the current rule is the one born in the second half of the registration period. Their achievement is relatively low because they are too immature. In turn, the efforts toward achieving the moral imperative disadvantage the achievement of our brightest and best. Therefore, the annual single-date-entry system negatively impacts academic achievement for the majority of our country's most valuable resource.

This chapter is about two "brass tacks"—delayed entry and dual entry—two fundamental concepts that can improve student achievement and, therefore, enhance potential for greater success. Coincidentally, they can improve student achievement while expending less money. Accomplishing improvement by innovating and actually reducing expenditures may seem paradoxical in the educational context, but accomplishing more with less is feasible.

The Finnish model of waiting until children are seven years of age may not fly in a world where both parents have to work and they are accustomed to an earlier entry age. The dual-entry model is a hybrid of two different worlds where children are grouped into six-month cohorts and where the majority of children are mature enough to engage successfully with formal learning. It also is a model where the potential of acceleration and deceleration to better meet students' educational needs can be achieved.

The data presented in this chapter would guarantee a huge savings or redeployment of about 4 percent of the annual operating budget while achieving a 5 percent improvement in student achievement for students born in the second half of the registration period. This latter point also results in a 60 percent reduction in student failure. Not calculated, at this point, is the gain in student success that would occur to our top-achieving students, who would no longer be constrained in their intellectual development by the glass ceiling effect brought about by education's pursuit of the moral imperative.

The key points made in this chapter are:

- Professional development only enjoys an enduring beneficial effect across a school if the administrators become involved and worked directly with teachers.
- Our kids get only one chance at an education and we need to get it right.
- Educational leadership has not been very diligent in weeding out poor performers or achieving change in weak classroom teachers.
- Children born near the end of the registration year face double jeopardy when they also are placed with teachers who are unable to support student achievement gains of at least one year.
- "High flier" students may actually achieve one grade level with a weak teacher, but their actual gain is less than expected.
- Out of frustration with slow progress in both removing and strengthening/helping weak teachers, the education system is focused on changing system practices.
- Even though the Finnish model for school entry at age seven would provide substantive savings, implementing it for North American society is unreasonable.
- A two-times-a-year entry system would be the elementary school's equivalent of the semester system which is widely used in secondary schools.
- Dual entry has the capacity for saving taxpayers a large sum of money while significantly improving educational outcomes.
- Dual entry has the capacity to facilitate acceleration and deceleration, while eliminating social promotion.
- Accomplishing more with less is feasible by adopting delayed entry and dual entry.

15

Getting Practical

DEALING WITH MISCONCEPTIONS

The previous chapter concluded with the notion that it is oxymoronic in education to talk about improvement in student outcomes based on less spending. The overwhelming sentiment in the education sector is that improvement requires keeping what is already in place and spending more. The culture is dominated by an attitude that "I am working very hard and unable to work any harder." Any thought that the work being undertaken is less effective or efficient is too readily dismissed.

While it was once popular to use the phrase "work smarter, not harder," this reform-minded thought is now generally discredited because people feel insulted that they might actually be engaged in an approach that is not the most up-to-date thinking. Hence the need to demonstrate in considerable detail the flawed practice of bringing students into the education system where the student cohort has a twelve-month age span. This chapter demonstrates in greater detail a simple change to this long-standing practice and how significant savings can be accrued. Or, if savings is not the objective, then it will demonstrate how money might be redeployed.

A relatively typical school-year model has students entering the school system for grade one in September of the registration period when they turn six. The major longitudinal study, which has served as the research backbone for this book, utilized a registration period of January 1 to December 31 for approximately half the districts; however, many of the smaller districts attempt to entice parents into their schools by allowing an extension from the December 31 date to the second February 28 date. The destructive nature of this provision has already been exposed.

The overarching rule is that parents must register their child for grade one if their child is six years of age by September 1. Children born after September 1 can be delayed until the next year; however, few children are held out of the school system because it has been the pattern for decades and because the need for custodial care is so great. Indeed, more than 96 percent of the region's children are enrolled in kindergarten in the year that they qualify by age for that program. From our study we can determine that more than 97 percent of these kindergarten students progress to grade one the following September.

In the previous chapter it became apparent that implementing a tweak to this existing model through a dual-entry approach is relatively minor in terms of operational implications. The tweak to the school year has students entering grade one on September 1 and on the following February 1. Children beginning on September 1 are all six years of age, having turned six between March 1 and August 31. Children beginning on February 1 turned six between September 1 and the following February 28.

Almost all of the children entering in this second cohort are six years of age prior to entering grade one. The small variance of having children entering on February 1 who turn six during that month is necessitated by the traditional school calendar with its two-month summer break. There are five school months in September to January and five school months in February to June.

In order to get five school months and have similar six-month cohorts, children born in February enter grade one when they are five years and eleven months of age. This is a relatively small tweak from the principle of starting school by six years of age necessitated by the school system's slavish use of two months of continuous vacation. This is another rule that can be readily altered in the event that starting school at age six is a priority.

People often think that the second entry group is expected to complete grade one by June, which is the end of the ten-month period for the September intake. Stated differently, there is the mistaken perception that children entering on February 1 will somehow have to cram the grade one program in by the end of June before the summer break. It is deeply engrained in our culture that a grade is completed in June.

People lose sight of the fact that twelve years of schooling are interrupted but not punctuated by twelve summer breaks. Learning is not that tidy. At the end of the first June in the traditional September to June school year, many students are not sufficiently ready from a learning perspective to progress to grade two, and many were ready to progress to grade two before the end of June.

The traditional approach merely uses the summer break as the signal point for regrouping students for another year of schooling. In that second year, there will be some students working at the grade two level, some at the grade three level and even beyond, and some still at the grade one level and even lower. Being grouped in the year two program is more a function of age than it is of intellectual development and academic achievement.

There is nothing magical about the twelve-grade concept other than it has been part of our culture for centuries. It can be changed. Indeed, some regions of North America have utilized a thirteenth year (grade thirteen) as the amount of time normally necessary to accommodate twelve grades of learning. Understanding this reality is absolutely necessary for understanding how simple it is to implement a dual-entry concept.

Therefore, students entering the second cohort for grade one beginning in February experience the summer break halfway through their grade, while those entering in September experience their summer break at the end of their grade. To assist in understanding how dual entry works across the school career of a student, it is helpful to think of the twelve-year school program as being comprised of twenty-four levels rather than twelve grades.

Both approaches provide the traditional twelve years of schooling, if educators continue to utilize the traditional instructional processes. If a student spends twelve years progressing through the twelve grades, the September entrant will graduate at the end of June while the February entrant will graduate at the end of January. The semester system, already in use, accommodates multiple graduation points during the traditional school year.

In the previous chapter we noted that the dual-entry approach provides a greater opportunity for students to have their time in the school system adjusted to their rate of learning. In the traditional approach with students registered in twelve-month cohorts, the school system is very reluctant to accelerate or decelerate the pace of student progress. Instituting a dual-entry concept allows for a more seamless transition from one cohort to another where the age differences between the cohorts are only six months rather than the traditional twelve.

DEMONSTRATING HOW DUAL-ENTRY SAVES TAXPAYERS

The previous chapter also outlined some of the savings which would result if governments and school districts adopted a dual-entry system. Having established this point, it is also necessary to discuss precisely what the term "savings" can mean. First and foremost, savings can truly be for the taxpayer when government is concerned about an existing deficit, debt, or the rate of taxation. In other words, the funding source, which is typically the government, has a priority to reduce its expenditures and make its services more efficient.

Figure 15.1 demonstrates how a school might be organized to achieve savings for the government. In this illustration, a school with four hundred students in grades one through six is depicted as being organized around twenty classes with approximately sixty-six students per grade. If a school board implemented a February entry to complement a September entry, and if it operated with the assumption that the government funding agency

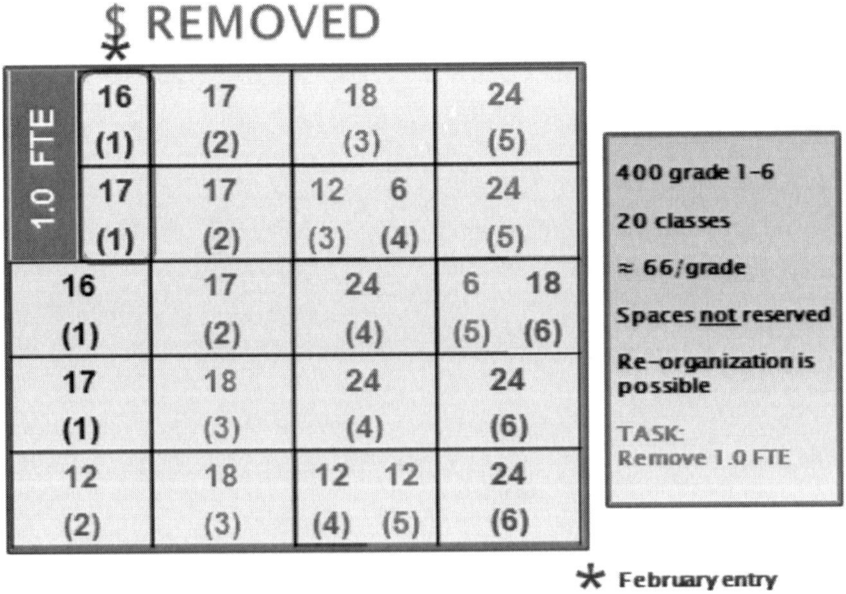

FIGURE 15.1.
Created by Jim Dueck.

required a savings, the school would function with the loss of one full-time classroom teacher.

In order to see how this would work, begin by calculating backward from grade six, where there would be two classes of twenty-four students in each class and a third class that would be split between grades five and six, with eighteen grade six students and six grade five students. Progressing through the grades in this model, note the organization for grade one on the left side of the chart. In dual entry for grade one, approximately thirty-three grade one students would begin in September and another thirty-three in February.

The September grade one student cohort is registered into two classes operating for the entire school year with seventeen students in one class and sixteen in the other. The two remaining boxes at the top of the left-hand column are reserved for the February entrants with seventeen students in one class and sixteen in the other. However, these two classes require teachers for only the second half of the school year, hence a savings of two half-time teachers for the school year.

Saving Money for Other School Purposes

If the school board operated with an assumption that the government funding agency did not require a savings, it could address alternative financial priorities. For example, the board could use the savings to improve the initial experience of first-graders. Grade one is considered a critical year for future academic success. Therefore government, or its school districts, might consider dramatic class-size reductions for grade one students by reserving spaces in classes during the September to January period for the February entrants.

Figure 15.2 depicts a similar set of parameters identified for the first use of savings demonstrated above, but without any effort by government to claw back the savings. In this example, by focusing on the grade one student placements in the left column, it is possible to see that there could be five classrooms with grade one students; however, one of the classrooms may be a split with twelve grade-two students and five of the more capable grade one students.

This fifth class, with some grade one students, allows for a reduction in class size for the rest of the school. In the four classes with only grade one students, each class would begin school in September with seven students and spaces reserved for eight or nine more students entering in the February cohort. In February all of these four grade one classes would have fifteen or

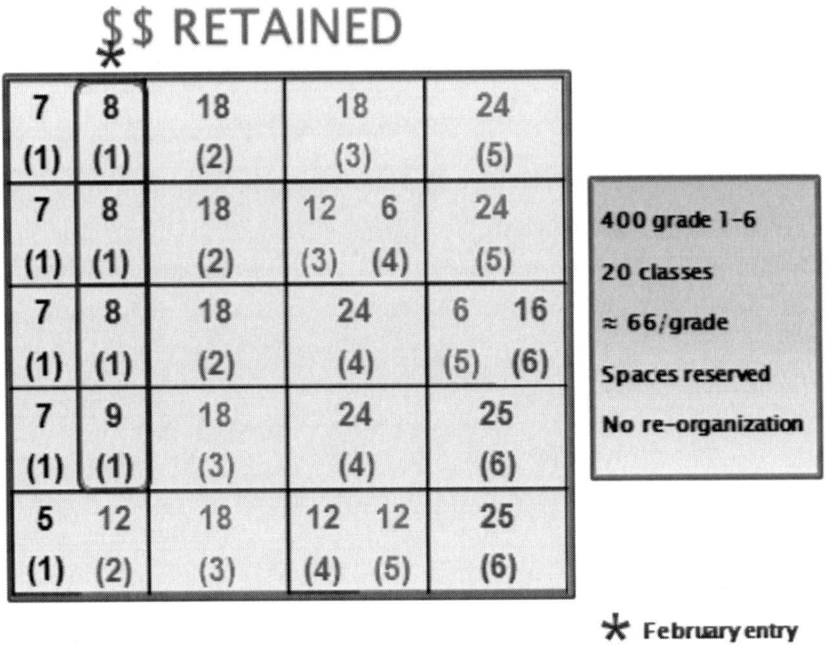

$$ RETAINED

7	8	18	18	24
(1)	(1)	(2)	(3)	(5)
7	8	18	12 6	24
(1)	(1)	(2)	(3) (4)	(5)
7	8	18	24	6 16
(1)	(1)	(2)	(4)	(5) (6)
7	9	18	24	25
(1)	(1)	(3)	(4)	(6)
5	12	18	12 12	25
(1)	(2)	(3)	(4) (5)	(6)

400 grade 1–6

20 classes

≈ 66/grade

Spaces reserved

No re-organization

✳ February entry

FIGURE 15.2.
Created by Jim Dueck.

sixteen students for the balance of the year. The teachers of these four classes would be employed for the entire year, and therefore the government or school board would not experience any financial benefit.

The above scenario depicted in figure 15.2 demonstrates just one use of savings by a school, but there are others. Many school districts now operate their schools more like a business by giving local schools control of their own budgets. It may be possible in a culture of overspending, which is an international problem, that a school needs to apply any savings it realizes to reduce or retire a budget deficit. Many governments around the world are in such a predicament, and it is likely that some schools find themselves in a similar situation.

Schools may also wish to invest in student programs for the gifted, or in enrichment programs to motivate students, or to address behavioral problems. Special interest programs, such as those associated with athletics or the arts, are often in need of operating money or money to acquire capital assets. There could also be a need in the classroom for a specialist teacher, who would rove from class to class to assist the regular classroom teacher in a specialist area such as mathematics.

In other words, there are many alternatives to setting aside space for February entrants. The point is that there is ample motivation at the school level to bring in a change like dual entry. It not only serves the primary purpose of the school, which is to provide the best possible education for every student in the fairest way possible, but it also provides the school with greater flexibility to pursue priorities that the staff believe would enhance the learning environment.

If the school makes no effort to reserve spaces for February entrants, it is likely that a significant portion of the school would experience a major reorganization in February in order to accommodate the new students. Many classes, for example, would be larger in the second term than in the first. These realities should not frighten administrators and teachers. The school has the prerogative to determine which course they wish to pursue. Choice in life is inevitable, and with it comes consequences which, in this case, are generally predictable and manageable.

The potential for midyear reorganization is the one downside of the dual-entry concept, and the school will need to approach it just as it approaches the beginning of school in September of the traditional school year. Unlike high schools, which operate on a semester system, elementary schools usually operate on a yearlong schedule, so the midyear reorganization will be more consequential.

And, while the school needs to give careful attention to the administrative details surrounding the reorganization, it should not lose sight of the big picture, which is about implementing reform that is for the benefit of the individual student and the school as a whole. Benefits, such as the reduction in the failure rate and an ability to meet the acceleration needs of the most capable students who are currently negatively impacted by the school's pursuit of the moral imperative, make the task of semiannual reorganization worthwhile.

Along with the educational benefits come financial benefits which have already been identified. Substantial savings accrue for the first twelve years and, along with them, there is a reduced cost associated with a dramatic decrease in the number of students that need ongoing remediation because of their poor start in grade one and the concomitant relative-age effect. These types of savings are ongoing.

There remains one other significant financial incentive for the funding agency. In education programs where student retention is practiced, many students are spending thirteen years in school instead of twelve. The cost of a thirteenth year imposes an additional demand on scarce resources to cover the additional year they are in school. This study, for example, demonstrated that 17 percent of students were retained in kindergarten to grade nine. The retention rate for students born in the first six months of the calendar was approximately 10 percent and 22 percent for those born in the second half of the year.

It is logical to conclude that the retention rates in a dual-entry program would be approximately equal for both cohorts. In this study, retention for the cohort of students entering in February would decrease from 22 percent to 10 percent. The cost to the government would decrease correspondingly, as far fewer students would need costly services. Not only would students require fewer classrooms, the school would also need fewer teachers to teach the additional year in school.

This chapter demonstrates the feasibility of implementing a dual-entry strategy for enhancing student success and reducing actual rates of student failure. It also demonstrates the mathematics behind greater efficiencies which translate into savings for the government and/or the school system. Perhaps most importantly, it clarifies that dual entry is not a radical or revolutionary concept that would be highly disruptive and anxiety filled. It employs a proven model, namely the "semester" system, and applies it to elementary schools where it is essentially unknown.

The key points made in this chapter are:

- The overwhelming sentiment in the education sector is that improvement requires keeping what is already in place and spending more.
- A dual-entry approach is relatively minor in terms of operational implications.
- Twelve years of schooling are interrupted but not punctuated by twelve summer breaks.
- The potential for midyear reorganization is the one downside of the dual-entry concept.
- Savings can truly be for the taxpayer when government is concerned about an existing deficit, debt, or the rate of taxation.
- Dual entry not only serves the primary purpose of the school, which is to provide the best possible education for every student in the fairest way possible, but it also provides the school with greater flexibility to pursue priorities that the staff believe would enhance the learning environment.

16

Dual Entry Is Not New

COURAGE NEEDS TO PREVAIL

In education it is somewhat axiomatic that there really are very few new ideas. Technology and being in the *age of intelligence* with scientific research are certainly helping to change negative features of this paradigm. Nevertheless, there have been many innovations, even in our lifetime, which reformers have attempted and schools have rejected simply because the timing was poor or there were too many challenges associated with implementation. Additionally, the law of inertia, a comfort with the "tried and proven," and a high regard for conformity have ensured that the system never adopted many worthy innovations.

One definition of cowardice is that it is the absence of courage. In an organizational context, the absence of courage is discretely disguised as conformity to the past and allegiance to the status quo. Provoking the education community to abandon its lethargy and timidity is an ongoing challenge for leadership. It will require tenacity and courage on the part of educational leaders if we are to end the long-standing practice of adhering to an annual single-date-entry system that features a twelve-month spread in age, and with that a concomitant spread in intellectual ability and emotional maturity.

A minister of education for the province of Ontario during turbulent times in the 1990s made an observation regarding the ongoing resistance to change evident in education. In exasperation during a television interview he stated that crisis was the only way to achieve educational change. This book exposes the crisis and calls for action. It is not that the crisis is new: it just has not been quantified, which is now feasible because we live in a time when people are well educated and capable of understanding a reasoned and reasonable argument based on scientific research. We are moving from having decisions based completely on intuition to an era where intelligence is also used.

Utilizing a dual-entry strategy as a means for neutralizing relative-age effect is not new. There have been at least two attempts to implement dual entry on a large scale, and both of these occurred in western Canada. Coincidentally this author was a participant in both attempts. Ultimately both were abandoned not because we found the theory to be deficient, but because we needed to invest more time and energy in implementation. The lessons are instructive for the future, and the failures show a way forward.

Calgary's Aborted Attempt

In the late 1960s and early 1970s, the Calgary Board of Education introduced dual-entry dates of September and February which remained in effect for five years before being abandoned. Even though this school district was one of the largest in the country, its initiative failed to inspire others, and the program operated somewhat as an anomalous "sore thumb": it was readily visible and, therefore, easily criticized as an experiment on children. It became apparent during this trial period that dual entry was a concept that served the interests of students well, but it was not necessarily in the best interest of other stakeholders.

Parents, for example, placed considerable emphasis on custodial care issues for their children. They viewed the school system as a convenient babysitting service, and they wanted their children in school as early as possible. The financial burden when the child is in the school system is not felt directly by the parents because it is shared among all taxpayers. Rule makers at the time heard a sufficient number of complaints from parents who were irritated by having to wait until their child was at least one half year older. In the 1960s, day-care programs were relatively few and generally expensive.

There was no data in those days as there is today to demonstrate the deleterious impact on young children when they start formal learning too early. Simply stated, there was no effort made to gather intelligence for decision making. Systematic testing of student achievement did not occur, and neither did an ongoing analysis of trends in student progress. There was not even any use of surveys to ascertain teacher or parent perceptions regarding the impact of this initiative. The education system was still functioning at the whim of a few loud voices: well-placed or shrilly expressed complaints could change policy direction, and they did.

Loud voices were also evident from an unexpected source within the educational community. The understanding of the project was that dual entry would be accompanied with dual exit, and students in elementary schools would exit to junior high schools both at the end of January and June. Semester schooling at that time was still a concept, and not happening, and dual exiting from an elementary school at the end of January meant that junior high school teachers had to reorganize classes to accommodate entry of students at the beginning of February.

This midyear incursion certainly was not convenient for a culture accustomed to a large group moving through the curriculum in lockstep tandem. Having multiple instructional groups operating in the same class was also not yet characteristic of high school programming. The textbook was the course; the course began on page one of the textbook, and everyone turned to page one on the same day and at the same time. The only variation that occurred related to which group students were assigned to, but regardless of the stream, all still worked with the same time frame and expectation.

Calgary's rule makers listened carefully to the loud complaints they received from middle school teachers faced with a potential midyear influx of students, and then responded by abandoning the initiative. During the fifth year of the project, with the lead group of students in grade five, rule makers instructed the system to manage student progress during the next year so that students would end grade six in June of the next school year or the one thereafter.

In other words, February-entering students would be either accelerated or decelerated by a half of a year to accommodate entry into grade seven the first year of Calgary's middle school program by the following September. The school district could have revised its strategy and made single exit by grade seven part of the initiative from that time forward, but they chose to respond to these two main concerns by abandoning the initiative entirely. Of course, using this approach would have really challenged the lockstep aspect of the grade system, where it was almost automatic that a child would not take less than six years to complete grades one through six.

British Columbia's Aborted Attempt

A second attempt to launch dual entry occurred several years later in another Canadian province of British Columbia (BC). The concerns about intellectual readiness, which gave rise to the initiative there, were similar to the ones raised in Calgary some twenty years earlier. However, the BC attempt was linked to several other initiatives in that province's Year 2000 project. Dual entry was but one component of a much larger reform effort.

One contentious initiative pertained to the elimination of report card marks, such as letter grades and percentages, which were to be replaced by use of documents referred to as "can do" reports. In the proposed format, parents would receive checklists of skills, knowledge, and abilities indicating what the child could do. Everyone was familiar with letter grades and percentages and, regardless of whether everyone had the same interpretation of what the letters or percentages meant, parents nevertheless had some understanding of how their child was progressing.

Public reaction to this change in reporting was swift and furious, resulting in dramatic intervention by the province's premier. His televised announcement that "Year 2000 is dead" resulted in the province hitting the "abort button" on all initiatives associated with Year 2000. Dual entry, which had just been introduced in pilot districts during an optional implementation year, was also terminated, along with a commitment from the minister of education that children entering the education system in February would be gradually synchronized with the September beginners by the end of grade three.

Thus another promising attempt ended in futility, although in this case the problems were not associated with the program, but with an educational environment over which it had no control. The issue remains unchanged: as long as a twelve-month age span remains, there will be students who are winners and losers based on something as simple as birth month and inadequate attention to family planning, and something as intransigent as our school system's slavish adherence to a long-standing rule.

The Calgary and BC attempts at reform illustrate that society is ready to consider dual entry, but they also point out that circumstances must be right and preparation must be thorough and intentional. In both cases, educators working with young children understood the issue, but there was no effort to quantify the problem so that parents could see the impact of the rules in place. Since these abortive attempts, large-scale standardized assessments and quantitative data are available. Armed with this information, educational leaders, politicians, and concerned parents are finally well positioned to make the necessary decisions and implement the changes. Leadership can no longer avoid making decisions.

The key points made in this chapter are:

- This book exposes the crisis and calls for action.
- There have been at least two attempts to implement dual entry on a large scale.
- There was no data in the previous attempts as there is today to demonstrate the deleterious impact on young children when they start formal learning too early.
- Previous attempts at implementing dual entry were unsuccessful due to political reasons and lack of preparation.

17

Conclusion

Speaking with educators and parents about relative-age effect almost always elicits the same response. People understand it because they have children impacted by this phenomenon or they have observed it in others. Certainly it is not new knowledge, but the fact that data is now available which demonstrates how many students are affected and the long-lasting implications generally catches most people by surprise. Indeed, it even catches educators by surprise.

In focus groups, parents quickly conceded that continuing with the current model is not in our society's best interests. They observed how important it is to be fair to the cohort of children currently labeled as immature so that they, too, might be successful. Just as parents teach their children to learn and mature, they believe the education system should learn from the data and change practice in the face of reasoned evidence. They recognize, however, that our culture may have to rethink the current paradigm which is having children begin school earlier, and that a change in practice will require regular, clear, substantial communication with the population.

Educators working in the lower grade levels recognize the issue from their experience in teaching young children. The current practices necessitated by the rules in place have been around for so long that the unfair outcomes identified in this book are now deemed acceptable. People are now desensitized to the tragedy because educators have implied that everything that can be done is being done. The wrongness of the situation is acceptable because life is not fair. Some will say, "I made it through and I am okay."

In the physical domain, Sidney Crosby may have been born in the eighth month (August) and Mario Lemieux in the eleventh (November), but they achieved hockey stardom. Some do overcome the odds because of exceptional talent or phenomenal environmental conditions such as being in homes where parenting is particularly effective or in classrooms where teaching is particularly skillful. Indeed life is not fair, and there are circumstances where environmental factors overcome the odds.

By the time students move into higher grades, teachers are rather un-likely to be aware that students struggling in their classrooms are victims of relative-age effect. Middle school teachers are simply too distant in time from the moment when parents had some choices regarding when to register their child, or the school had a responsibility for providing parents with some timely counseling about registering their child prematurely. Besides, the data demonstrated that many of the students born in the latter half of the registration year have already failed by the time they are in middle school and are, therefore, unlikely to be failed a second time.

Further, relative-age effect is a generalization and not a rule. One principal likened this situation to current laws regarding the use of seat belts in cars. Even though many more people survive a crash when wearing a belt, everybody knows someone who was not wearing one during a crash and yet survived without much injury. Similarly, there are hockey players born in the last quarter of the year who perform well in the NHL. In school, there are some students who do well regardless of when they were born in the registration year. There is some risk involved when recommending action on generalizations.

When school district trustees viewed this information, they too were taken by surprise. They described this as "seismic" and wondered how they should proceed. Their query was whether pilot projects should be launched. It is doubtful that a few districts piloting an initiative could overcome the pressure from parents wanting their child in the school system as early as possible. Their approach would be to heap scorn upon the school district for experi-menting with their child, or they would do everything possible to find another school where they could enroll earlier than later.

In the sports domain there appears to be general acceptance of the relative-age effect, and little impetus for change. Sport is big business in the entertainment industry, and competition is fierce. Perhaps the nature of this domain leads people to believe that it is an optional aspect of life where survival of the fittest, or biggest, is entirely appropriate. There are enough participants in the limited market to meet the demand. After all, it is not necessary that every aspirant be successful.

Or, because education also follows a twelve-month registration window, why would parents and organizers contemplate pushing for change within the sports domain? After all, if the education community thinks the approach is acceptable, why should the sports domain push for a change? Perhaps educators need to be courageous and become the "push for change" which reduces unfairness to our society's children.

Needs are entirely different in the educational domain, and placing a significant percentage of children at risk over such a simple matter should be unacceptable. Fairness is important, and treating children equitably is a touchstone of our society. If we believe that children are a nation's most valuable resource, it certainly seems paramount to our future success that we do whatever we can to ensure that each student is able to maximize his or her potential.

Having moved into the *age of intelligence* where we are now equipped with information about an unfair situation perpetrated by our rules of the day, and then not undertaking an appropriate response, seems uncaring, even irresponsible. The fact that so many students are actually retained or failed in at least one grade during their school years for no other reason than they entered the formal learning process at the younger end of the age continuum, is a tragedy.

The fact that so many other students are also impacted by either having to undertake significant remediation because they were able to stay above the retention threshold, or because their educational needs are being sacrificed in order to focus on the weaker end of the continuum, adds to the tragedy of those actually being retained. The irony in these tragedies is that strategies are available to overcome the relative-age effect, which actually achieves better educational results with a significant cost savings.

It is important to understand that it is the interplay of two factors that makes the relative-age effect a significant issue. Having children participate in formal learning activity before intellectual maturity warrants can be deleterious to a child. Developing a healthy self-esteem is critical for ongoing success. Combining the second factor of placing very young students in a cohort that includes a twelve-month spread in ages exacerbates this situation. We are naïve if we do not think that children are very aware of how they are progressing relative to peers.

Certainly the data is now building for parents to understand that children born in the latter portion of a twelve-month registration period potentially face a double whammy. Gladwell demonstrated how the physical dimension is negatively impacted, and this book demonstrates a similar effect in the intellectual domain. However, the physical domain does not have the impact on a nation's success as does the intellectual domain.

There is also a difference in the context of the two domains. In the physical domain, the older, faster, bigger, and stronger children benefit from their talent by being substantially enriched by contact with superior coaches or being placed with other super-talented players. In education, however, the focus is more on the struggling students with the result that the more talented are actually held back from achieving their potential. The significant difference between the two domains is that in the intellectual or educational domain, everyone remains in the program, and success for all is seen as a vital resource for our nation.

There is an inherent motivation within the educator community to ameliorate the disadvantages facing the weaker students more than there is for dealing with the challenges required in ensuring that exceptional students are the recipients of educational programming that will motivate them in maximizing their potential. In effect, remediation trumps enrichment in our schools' emphasis, and there is a subliminal mindset occurring that "dumbs down" the classroom curriculum.

Options for transforming education have been identified. Finland's success demonstrates that less can be more; however, the cultural shift required may be too difficult to introduce in today's economic environment. Multiple entry points, even if only two, can ameliorate the negative effects of grouping students with too wide a range in ability. This approach also raises the intellectual age or maturity with which children enter formal learning. It also introduces the chances of having greater flexibility in accommodating acceleration or deceleration of student progress.

These options introduce an interesting issue in education and for the political entities that govern and operate our school systems. Specifically, doing the right thing in the interest of fairness to our nation's children can actually be accomplished without huge additional expenditures of taxpayer resources. Significant savings are available.

Today's rules in education are well entrenched in a system that is loath to change. Hopefully by exposing data in such a large study, parents and educators will unite in a movement that sweeps away intransigence and brings transformational change. Birth rather than worth is counting too much; it has brought about an unfair situation that research has starkly exposed as untenable and unconscionable. Gladwell's words bear repeating:

> We could easily take control of the machinery of achievement . . . but we don't. And why? Because we cling to the idea that success is a simple function of individual merit and that the world into which we all grow up and the rules we choose to write as a society don't matter at all.

Somehow Gladwell's words need to be changed. The focus on education is increasing as politicians begin to understand its importance to a nation's future prosperity and as they become frustrated with spending more without seeing more. On February 28, 2010, President Obama gave a speech to the US Chamber of Commerce where he emphasized his commitment to students by outlining his strategy to ensure that appropriate pressure would be applied.

The *New York Times'* report of his speech the next day summarized the president's vision with the words, "President Obama said Monday that he favored federal rewards for local school districts that fire underperforming teachers and close failing schools, saying educators needed to be held accountable when they failed to fix chronically troubled classrooms and curb the student dropout rate." The president was focused on teachers, obviously, but it is logical that he would be similarly inclined if the evidence was showing that rule makers were not demonstrating their courage by reform.

In education, the opposite of courage is conformity. Hopefully the evidence compiled in this book will provide sufficient courage to prompt rule makers toward a transformational change where very young children will no longer be subjected to an annual single-date-entry system which places them in an end-of-year birth month. Or, if the system chooses to continue with an unfair situation for these children, parents will understand that knowing the month to become pregnant is a vital aspect of good parenting.

The key points made in this chapter are:

- How many students are affected and the long-lasting implications of our current system generally catch most people, including educators, by surprise.
- Some people think the wrongness of the current situation is acceptable because life is not fair.
- Relative-age effect is a generalization and not a rule.
- Now that we are equipped with information about an unfair situation perpetrated by our rules of the day, not undertaking an appropriate response seems uncaring, even irresponsible.
- Doing the right thing in the interest of fairness to our nation's children can actually be accomplished without huge additional expenditures of taxpayer resources.
- Birth rather than worth is counting too much.
- Fairness to children requires change in practice from either the school system or parents.

References

Alexander, K. L., Entwisle, D. R., and Olson, L. S. "Schools, achievement, and inequality: A seasonal perspective." *Educational Evaluation and Policy Analysis*, 23(2), 171 91. CAT-V N=665, CAT-M N=678.

Argenti, D. (2010, August 12). "Require kindergarteners to be 5 by Sept. 1." *San Francisco Chronicle*. Retrieved from http://www.sfgate.com/opinion/openforum/article/Require-kindergarteners-to-be-5-by-Sept-1-3178868.php.

Barber, M., and Mourshed, M. *How the world's best-performing school systems come out on top*. New York: McKinsey and Company, 2007.

Barber, M. *Instruction to deliver*. London: Methuen Pub. Ltd., 2008.

Byrd, R. S., Weitzman, M., and Auinger, P. "Increased behavior problems associated with delayed school entry and delayed school progress." *Pediatrics, 100*(4), 654–61.

Cascio, E., and Schanzenbach, D. *First in the class? Age and the education production function*. National Bureau of Economic Research, 1050 Massachusetts Avenue, Cambridge, MA 02138, USA 2008.

Crosser, S. "Summer birth date children: Kindergarten entrance age and academic achievement." *Journal of Educational Research*, 84, 140–6.

Deming, D., and Dynarski, S. *The lengthening of childhood* (NBER Working Paper No. 14124). 2008.

Fullan, M. *The moral imperative of school leadership.* Thousand Oaks, CA: Corwin Press Inc., 2003.

Gladwell, M. *Outliers.* New York: Little, Brown and Company, 2008.

Goodman, R. *Child psychiatric disorder and relative age within school year.* London: BMJ Publishing Group Ltd., 2003.

Goodman, R., Gledhill, J., and Ford, T. (2003). *Child psychiatric disorder and relative age within school year: Cross sectional survey of large population sample.* BMJ Publishing Group Ltd., 2008.

Hawerchuk, D. *Junior hockey and age, part 1.* World Wide Web. 2011.

Juel, C., Biancarosa, G., Coker, D., and Deffes, R. "Walking with Rosie: A cautionary tale of early reading instruction." *Educational Leadership,* 60, 12–18.

Laurie, R. *Grade inflation sets up students to fail: Study.* Halifax, Nova Scotia: Atlantic Institute for Marketing, 2007.

Leuven, E., Lindahl, M., Oosterbeek, H., and Webbink, D. *New evidence on the effect of time in school on early achievement.* Mimeo, Universiteit van Amsterdam, 2003.

Mashburn, A. J., and Pianta, R. C. "Social relationships and school readiness." *Early Education & Development,* 17, 151–76.

Mauldin, J., and Tepper, J. *Endgame.* Hoboken, NJ: John Wiley and Sons Inc., 2011.

Mayer, S., and Knutson, D. (1999). *Does the timing of school affect how much children learn?* In S. Mayer and P. Peterson (Eds.), *Earning and learning: How schools matter* (pp. 79–102). Washington, DC: Brookings Institution Press.

McGrath, M. J. (2007). *Performance evaluation: Tenure—Ain't it awful!* Retrieved from http://www.mcgrathinc.com/Articles/PerformEval1.html.

Mendleson, R. "Why it's so hard to fire bad teachers." *Macleans,* July 8, 2009.

Nir, S. (2011, February 15). "Reading at some private schools is delayed." *New York Times,* p. A21.

Sharp, C., Hutchison, D., and Whetton, C. "How do season of birth and length of schooling affect children's attainment at key stage 1?" *Educational Research,* 36(2), 107–21.

Shepard, L. A., and Smith, M. L. (1986). "Synthesis of Research on School Readiness and Kindergarten Retention." *Educational Leadership,* 44, 78–86.

Sparks, D. (2001). "Why change is so challenging for schools: An interview with Peter Senge." *Journal of Staff Development*, 22(3).

Sprietsma, M. (2007). "The effect of relative age in the first grade of primary school on long-term scholastic results: International comparative eidence using PISA 2003." ZEW Discussion Papers, No. 07-037, http://hdl.handle.net/10419/24601.

Strom, B. "Schooling and human capital in the global economy: Revisiting the equity-efficiency quandary." CESifo/PEPG Conference, Munich, September 2004.

Thomas, D., and Bainbridge, W. "Grade inflation: The current fraud." *Effective School Research.* January 1997.

Thompson, A. H., Barnsley, R. H., and Dyck, R. J. "A new factor in youth suicide: The relative age effect." *Canadian Journal of Psychiatry*, 44, 82–5.

Webber, C., Aitken, N., Lupart, J., and Scott, S. *The Alberta student assessment study.* The Crown in Right of Alberta, 2009.

Weisberg, D., Sexton, S., Mulhern, J., and Keeling, D. *The widget effect: Our national failure to acknowledge and act on differences in teacher effectiveness.* New York: The Carnegie Corporation of New York, 2009.

Woods, M. (2008, September 19). "Making the grade." *Queen's Journal*, 136(8).

Xiang, Y., Dahlin, M., Cronin, J., Theaker, R., and Durant, S. "Do high performing students maintain their altitude?" *Performance Trends of Top Performing Students.* Thomas B. Fordham Institute, September 20, 2011.

About the Author

Jim Dueck, EdD, has had a career in education spanning forty years of service as a teacher, principal, superintendent, and assistant deputy minister. He has also advised representatives from almost fifty education systems around the world who have sought suggestions regarding assessment and accountability in education, including the US government's launch of the Race to the Top initiative.